When Men and
Mountain Meet

*I dedicate this book to the memory of my parents,
Y Parchedig / The Reverend Gwyn Eifion Rees
and Betty Jones, Rhosfa*

When Men and Mountain Meet

THE STORY OF THE
BLACK MOUNTAIN ROAD

ALDWYTH REES DAVIES

First impression: 2019

© Copyright Aldwyth Rees Davies and Y Lolfa Cyf., 2019

Cover photograph: Aldwyth Rees Davies
Cover design: Y Lolfa

ISBN: 978 1 78461 751 6

Published and printed in Wales
on paper from well-maintained forests by
Y Lolfa Cyf., Talybont, Ceredigion SY24 5HE
website www.ylolfa.com
e-mail ylolfa@ylolfa.com
tel 01970 832 304
fax 832 782

Preface

IN 2019 IT will be 200 years since the road across the Black Mountain (Mynydd Du), the A4069 from Brynaman to Llangadog, was constructed. Featured in many motoring journals, this has been described as one of the best roads to drive on in Wales.

The road came into being because of the efforts of a father and son, both named John Jones. In addition, they could also be regarded as the founding fathers of Brynaman itself. Their story is complex however, as, because they had exactly the same name, they were often confused as one man. Theirs is a *riches* to *rags* story. John Jones the son built a house which gave its name to Brynaman, and folklore suggests that he may have lost the house later in a bet.

Construction of the road over the Black Mountain led to increased industrialisation in the area and changed this small corner of Wales for ever. Other consequences of the road are links to the Rebecca Riots, the railway mania of the 1840s, coal mining and quarrying, cholera, Nonconformity, and the success of the Welsh language. The Black Mountain area of Wales was very remote before this father and son brought the road, and later the railway, to the region. This book is a celebration of their achievements.

I have attempted to bring together in one place pieces of information from numerous archives, libraries, old newspapers and other sources. My aim is to offer interesting facts rather than an in-depth analysis of the topics covered. Several books already assess the history of the Amman Valley coal-mining area but I haven't come across any that deal with the road.

Interrelated events have left a permanent mark on the history, landscape and people of this small area of Wales. As in poet William Blake's line, 'Great things are done when men and mountains meet'.[1]

***

I would like to thank Treftadaeth Brynaman / Brynamman Heritage group and all its members, contributors and volunteers who busily preserve artefacts, for kindly sharing their information with me.

I am also very grateful to Glyn Jones, a descendant of the Jones family and co-author of *In the Mist of Time*[2], for letting me have a copy of his book so that checking facts didn't warrant a personal 200-mile round trip to visit West Glamorgan Archives in Swansea. His volume is an invaluable source of information for anyone interested in the Jones family tree and it includes some photographs. I only discovered this book late in my research but it helped to confirm some events. Enoch Rees's book, *Hanes Brynaman* (1896), was a good source of information about the period from 1819 to 1896, and was written as a result of oral information. Another interesting book was *Hanes Eglwys Cwmllynfell* [History of Cwmllynfell Church] by Owen, James & Davies (1935).

I would also like to acknowledge the friendly and helpful staff at the National Library of Wales in Aberystwyth.

There I found an informative contemporary source, an unpublished essay by a 28-year-old local man, Daniel Williams of Cwmteg, who wrote it a few years before he died in 1869.[3] Finding John Jones Senior's will, dated 1835, was also valuable.

My thanks too to the staff at West Glamorgan Archives and Library in Swansea who made visiting and finding documents a pleasure.

I was unable to find any original plans or records that John Jones made about the road, as details of the construction work have not survived, according to M.C. Evans writing 'Forgotten Roads of Carmarthenshire' in *The Carmarthenshire Antiquary* journal. However, the greatest discovery for me was coming across an original hand-drawn sketch at the British Library, dated 1826. This sketch was made for the first ever Ordnance Survey maps in the 1830s. This, I believe, is the first time the Black Mountain road was ever recorded on any map. I came across the sketch after hours of looking through boxes, as the search was made harder because Brynaman/ Gwter Fawr and the road itself go through different county and parish lines: Glamorgan and Carmarthenshire, and Llangadog, Llandeilo Fawr and Llangiwig parishes. I must therefore thank the staff in the Map Room of the British Library for their patience in bringing up box after box from their strongrooms for me to search through, as there was no definitive shelf number for this drawing. The British Library has kindly given me permission to include a photograph of the relevant section.

In researching this book I have come to feel very indebted to numerous unnamed people who must have spent an uncountable number of hours transcribing old documents and creating websites we can all use. Gareth Hicks's work on the genuki.org.uk website has been especially invaluable as a catapult to further research.

Also, I'd like to thank the current owner of Brynaman House who is taking such good care of this old, historically important house.

My final gratitude goes to Y Lolfa for all their work, and to my family for all their encouragement.

It was after the funeral of a relative in 2012 that I started my research. My daughter Ffion asked me who were all the people filling Bethania Chapel in Rhosaman that day. When I replied that she was related in some way to most of them, as her four grandparents came from the area, I realised that I needed to research and record some family history for her and her brothers, Gareth and Rhys. This then led to researching the history of an area I thought I knew. It took me off the beaten track, both physically and mentally, and led to undiscovered walks and the excitement of finding a new piece of information in old documents. One of the more memorable experiences was coming across an old cemetery in Cwmllynfell. Hidden amongst old woods, brambles and ivy, I found John Jones Senior's gravestone. At that moment, crossing over an old bridge out of the almost forgotten cemetery, I decided to write this work for publication, so that there is some record and celebration of the story of these pioneering men.

As a family we have never lived in Wales, but have resided in Belgium, South Africa and England. However, many summer holidays involved visits to Brynaman and travelling over the Black Mountain road. I have personally

8

never lived in Brynaman either, but both my parents did and, therefore, whenever anyone asks me which part of Wales I come from, I always say Brynaman.

Aldwyth Rees Davies
May 2019

Contents

CHAPTER 1

Pre-industrial history

THE BLACK MOUNTAIN and its road connect two very different parts of Wales, the agrarian or agricultural north and the industrial south. In order to build a picture of what the Black Mountain area looked like before industrialisation, there follows a brief account of its history up until then.

If you drive on the mountain road today and look over Brynaman, it's hard to believe that it was once a very rural, remote place. In contrast, if you look north towards the Gwynfe side of the mountain, the difference now is striking, with its still patchwork-quilt effect of fields, no industry or any other development to be seen. It remains as it has always been – an agricultural area. But Brynaman, despite the Industrial Revolution, did not grow into a town but, rather, a large village in a long linear pattern.

The northern side of the Black Mountain (Gwynfe)

The northern aspect of the Black Mountain has an ancient history. Gwynfe is the first village you reach as you head north and drive over and down the mountain and enter the enclosed field system. Gwynfe village is now off to the left of the main road, although an old turnpike road used to go through Gwynfe itself, and on to the tollgate located on the lower reach of the mountain. Gwynfe dates back to at least medieval times, and still has its small church (now decommissioned) which dates from the 16th century. The parish of Gwynfe has remained an agricultural area accessed only by narrow country roads, with the occasional farm, mostly 19th century. The commoners of Gwynfe and also nearby Myddfai have a long history of grazing rights on the Black Mountain. There is evidence that the area has been farmed since the Middle Ages.[1]

Thirteenth-century Carreg Cennen Castle is visible from the surrounding countryside and from the old turnpike road on the Black Mountain. The castle sits on top of a very steep limestone crag and dominates the landscape. Many artists have been inspired to paint it and, in 1798, J.M.W. Turner, when he was about 23, made a sketch of Carreg Cennen Castle which is now held at Tate Britain in London.[2]

The first castle on the site was probably a wooden structure built by the Lord Rhys, Prince of Deheubarth, in the 12th and 13th centuries, although there is some evidence of earlier prehistoric occupation. One legend suggests that the original fortress dates back to the Dark Ages and reign of King Arthur and belonged to the Welsh Lord of IsCenen, Urien Rheged and his son Owain.

An interesting account of the castle, written in 1462, is attributed to Urien, Lord IsCenen:

> Having maintained there a garrison during the summer of the
> Yorkists decided in the August to demolish the rocky fortress
> which was so strong that no one dared approach it and had
> been the haunt of rebels and robbers intent on the destruction
> of the country side. Five hundred men with bars, picks and

crowbars of iron were engaged in its destruction to avoid inconvenience of the kind in future.[3]

Luckily, they didn't succeed in its complete destruction and disappearance – as they left a magnificent picturesque ruin.

This side of the Black Mountain has changed very little pre- and post-industrialisation, compared to the Brynaman side, and offers an amazing view as you travel over the summit on the mountain road.

The southern side of the Black Mountain (Brynaman)

Brynaman, a large village on the southern side of the Black Mountain, lies to the west of the Brecon Beacons and is divided into Upper and Lower Brynaman. The boundary between them is the River Amman which flows at the bottom of Station Road. The river is also the boundary between the counties of Carmarthenshire and West Glamorgan. There is evidence that people have lived in this area for centuries, as there are ruins of ancient stone dwellings, possibly prehistoric, as well as early types of limekilns and medieval rectangular buildings on the mountain's lower slopes. Brynaman's close neighbours, Gwaun-Cae-Gurwen to the west and Rhosaman and Cwmllynfell to the east, all have evidence of human occupation going far back into history. There is proof of circular and oval-shaped houses, land clearance, linear boundaries on the slopes of the mountain, and some medieval or post-medieval house foundations.

The first buildings in the wider area were on the steep

slopes of the upper valley of the River Garw, and were built using the many loose stones left by an early glacier. Shepherds from large farms, owned by barons living in the more fertile Towy Valley, brought their herds onto the mountain for summer pasture. Herdsmen would make primitive shelters to keep themselves dry and warm, using whatever was at hand: rocks for walls; gorse, heather and grass as roofing. The foundations of other larger rectangular buildings can be found near the River Garw. This indicates that these shepherds either stayed for longer periods or made more permanent dwellings. There are signs of walled enclosures used as animal pounds and areas of land possibly used for growing food. According to an archaeological study of the Black Mountain, there is little evidence of associated field boundaries, but what has been found is probably more associated with a pastoral economy.[4] Also on the southern slopes, near the old turnpike road which is now a footpath, there is a large example of a complex enclosure – a group of the footings of different buildings in close proximity.

The upper region of the Black Mountain has no trees nowadays and this probably has been so for centuries, which would have made it easier for shepherds to keep watch over their flocks, of course. It was quite the opposite on the lower slopes, which had a thick forest of trees covering the whole valley floor. The land gradually began to be farmed but, generally, the Amman Valley was very slow to develop. It is not clear what kind of relationship farmers had with the barons who supposedly owned these great expanses of land which they had acquired through battle, marriage or inheritance. Many farms were recorded in the lordships' account books, so it is presumed that taxes of some sort were paid. It is known that this area was used by lords for hunting in the 17th century. A lodge called Noyadd Wen, located between Brynaman and Garnant, was used for this purpose, and once belonged to Sir Rhys ap Thomas of Dinefwr (1449–1525). There is a record of a farm called Gorshelig that formed part of the boundary of land owned by the Lord of Gower. It sits near a peatbog which is the source of two brooks, one flowing east towards the River Llynfell and the other flowing west into the River Amman at Rhosaman.[5]

Footpaths or tracks between these early farms would have been the first routes on the mountain. An old map, made by English map engraver Emanuel Bowen in 1729, shows such routes in the area, one being from Carreg Cennen Castle and which forded the River Amman near Glanaman and then crossed the Betws mountain to the town of Neath. This route would have allowed access to the Amman Valley.

As small farms began to be established on land adjacent to the River Amman, farmers would have discovered the coal dug up whilst ploughing the land. Coal near the surface of land was absent on the Gwynfe side, so Amman Valley farmers may have started selling it to farmers on the other side of the mountain, possibly swapping it for lime which was spread on fields as fertiliser. They would have walked, then used mules or horses to transport the heavy minerals along rough tracks.

With limestone kilns having been opened on the lower northern slopes of the mountain around 1750, large quantities of coal were needed for fuel. When coal was dug up, iron was found too, and mining became a large-scale operation in the area.

At the turn of the 19th century, according to an account written in 1865 by Daniel Williams who lived on a local farm called Cwmteg, inhabitants of the small scattered farms around the settlement of Gwter Fawr (which is called Brynaman these days) would have carried coal over the mountain to the kilns in summer, and to the houses of Gwynfe in winter. Each farm would have had up to seven horses or mules to carry the coal. The coal wasn't sourced in deep mines at this time but in outcrop workings where it was found nearer to the surface. Water from rivers was used to wash away any waste material. This is the origin of the name Gwter Fawr (Big Gutter).

In 1610, during the reign of James I, a baron court was held at Noyadd Wen when the tenants of Kaegurwen, then an ancient manor that included present-day Gwaun-Cae-Gurwen and what is now Lower Brynaman, held the rights to the coal that lay under their land. What is surprising about this is that the tenants, not the landowner, held the rights. The baron court's adjudication stated: 'the coal and seams below the ground in the possession of a tenant, were owned by the tenant and not by the landlord, and that the tenant could dig, excavate and sell the coal without the permission of the owner of the land.'[6]

Looking at adverts published in local newspapers between 1804 and 1919, it is interesting to note that some farm sales specifically state that 'all mineral content' is included in the sale.[7] Some people came to realise that there was money to be made, so they bought local farmland for its mineral content.

One such man was John Jones of Brynbrain Farm, Cwmllynfell, near Brynaman. He purchased a large amount of property on the southern side of the mountain in the early 1800s. With his son, also called John, he started to transform the upper Amman Valley from a farming area into an industrial one. Farming on the southern side of the mountain became more of a second livelihood as men earned more working in the mines than on farms.

Contrast this to the Glamorgan coalfields where the landlords of the Rhondda 'according to English Law owned the minerals beneath the soil'[8] of their estates. They, therefore, received royalties for all the coal mined on their land which explains the readiness of the old landowning class to cooperate with the new industrialists. This accounts for the wealth accumulated by, for example, the Marquis of Bute who was the principal landowner in Glamorgan.

But, in Brynaman and in the surrounding area, the ownership of coal mines started off as small-scale enterprises with a single owner, or perhaps a few people joining together to open mines. These businesses often changed hands, and no one man owned all of the land or industries.

Although coal and iron extraction has left its scars on the Black Mountain landscape, nature is gradually recovering nowadays. The remaining quarry ruins are only visible from the northern side – looking now like natural crags from a distance. The remainder of the mountain is a wide expanse of upland moor, uninhabited apart from grazing sheep. Scattered farmhouses are to be found on the hillsides. Poor-quality soil meant that people eked out their living on farms.[9] And it was probably poverty that made farmers try to cultivate the barren uplands, thus increasing the demand for lime to improve the soil. And lime, fortunately, could be found on top of the Black Mountain.

The Limestone Quarries

Black Mountain limestone has been quarried for use in agriculture, building work and industry. Traces of limestone quarrying (be it quarry workings, limekilns, or spoil heaps) go back hundreds of years, from small-scale local exploitation in the 18th century and before, to larger industrial use in the 20th century. The last large quarry on the summit was called Herbert's Quarry.

The Black Mountain was part of the vast Vaughan and Cawdor estate, whose ancestral home was Gelli Aur / Golden Grove, near Llandeilo. These lords of the land issued leases for quarrying on the Black Mountain but many tenant farmers considered the unenclosed mountain land as being their 'right of common' – something which dated back to medieval times. Documents from 1755 show that farmers were secretly making lime and selling it without the estate's permission. Evidence of early small earth and stone kilns can be found on the northern slopes between Tro'r Gwcw (more about this iconic name in the next chapter) and the old turnpike road.

In the 18th century great changes were happening in agriculture on the northern side of the mountain, thus increasing production and efficiency. Lime played an important part in this as it was used as a soil improver. New land could be brought into cultivation to help increase crop yields. There was great poverty in rural areas at this time, and the ever-growing population in the countryside was desperate for food. But the demands of nearby developing industrial areas also needed to be met, as lime was a valuable commodity to them as well. The lime and coal industry became linked with the formation of the Llangadog Trust in 1779, whose main purpose was to improve access to the limekilns on the mountain and the coal in the valley below.

Limestone, broken up into small pieces, burned with coal which then turned it to a usable soil improver. Coal was used because of the duration it could burn; it would not get crushed by the weight of the limestone above it, either. One ton of coal was needed to produce one ton of quicklime, the usable end product.

As the lime industry expanded rapidly due to increase in demand, the only way to transport it down the Black Mountain was by cart. The first carts in the area were described as sledges; these were later replaced by wheeled carts.[10] A procession of horse-drawn carts must have been quite a frequent sight going up and down the mountain on both sides. In 1854 travel writer George Borrow described the noise they made as he descended down the mountain to Gwter Fawr (now Brynaman), a place he planned to stay the night at after a long walk on the mountain:

> I heard a noise, as if a number of carts were coming rapidly down the hill. I stopped… the noise drew nearer… horses, carts, and forms of men passing. In one or two cases the wheels appeared to be within a few inches of my feet. I let the train go by, then called, am I right for Gutter Vawr?[11]

A long line of lime carts in rainy weather would churn up the country tracks as, being heavier, they did more damage than any other vehicle. It was a dangerous job carting the lime up and down the mountain. Newspapers in the 19th century often reported accidents to workers or drivers, with men and boys being thrown off or falling under the wheels of carts. A memorial stone lies near the quarries; it has an inscription to a lad from Gwynfe who had such an accident in 1884. Those in charge of the carts would blow horns to warn others as they tried to speed along the tracks. Later, a traction engine was used by the Brynaman Silica Company to carry stone they quarried at Pen y Rhiw Wen on the southern side of the mountain. This was a heavy, steam engine and a photograph of it is to be found in *Amman Valley Long Ago* (1987).

The distance some of the workers travelled from their homes to the quarries meant that they stayed on-site 24 hours a day, living in tents and outhouses during the week and going home only on Sundays. In winter, because of severe weather on the mountain, there was no work at the quarries. Even at other times of the year, working on a high, exposed summit meant the weather was always changeable. It could be wet, windy and cold, which must have made working conditions hard most of the time as the men quarried and cut stone into the smaller pieces necessary for tipping into kilns. A more dangerous job, with serious health consequences, was collecting processed lime from the bottom of the kilns after firing, and then carrying it to the carts waiting outside. They only had pieces of cloth to cover their faces. The possibility of the wind blowing the lime back into the workers' eyes, mouth and nose was constant as the wind travelled up from the valley below.

Nowadays you can visit the quarries and look into one kiln which still has its workings intact. It looks as if the quarrymen have just left, leaving the lime to drip down. It has, of course, calcified, and an iron gate blocks the entry for safety reasons. When the quarry was at full capacity the scene from the Gwynfe side must have been quite impressive, or foreboding, depending on your point of view!

The last quarry closed in 1958. Dyfed Archaeological Trust's 'Calch' project has an excellent webpage and free booklet on the history of the lime quarries.[12]

Geology of the Black Mountain

It took millions of years to create the various strata or seams of different minerals and stones laid down on the Black Mountain. It's hard to imagine that the area was once in the southern tropics and part of coastal plains. At that time Old Red Sandstone was formed, which is what most of the Black Mountain is made up of. The area was then covered by sea. (Nowadays, fossils of sea creatures or organisms can be found in the debris of the old quarries in between layers of carboniferous limestone.) Then there followed a period when thick, coarse sand was deposited. Known as Twrch Sandstone, this is now the hard rock found on the southern side of the mountain.[13]

A series of ice ages also left their mark on the Black Mountain. Glacier till, which is a combination of boulders and clay covering more solid rock, is scattered all over the mountain. Even as far down as Gwaun-Cae-Gurwen Common (near the footpath that leads to Hermon Chapel), there is a very large rock known as 'Carreg Sylfaen'; it was probably left there by a glacier.

The warmer climates which followed resulted in the formation of peatbogs. One of these peat areas is called

'Banc y Cerrig Pwdron', which translates as 'bank of the rotten stones', and can be seen to the east of the old turnpike road near the summit of Garreg Fraith. These 'stones' are, in fact, earth mounds of three-to-four feet high.

Another layer of the mountain is thick sandstone called Farewell Rock. It was given this name because no coal worth working could be found beneath this stratum. Ironstone miners first used the term when they found that digging deeper would not produce more areas of iron ore, so it was 'farewell' to further riches. The name was subsequently adopted by colliers in search of coal. This rock forms the base of the coal seam which starts on the lower southern slopes of the mountain where Brynaman, Rhosaman and Cwmllynfell are situated.

This hard-wearing rock was crushed to make silica bricks. In some parts this sandstone naturally weathered to produce silica sand, which was also exploited by industry. Silica sand was used to make firebricks and line furnaces in the metal industries of Swansea and Merthyr Tydfil. A limestone and silica quarry was located at the previously mentioned Pen y Rhiw Wen, a little further south of the summit.

So plenty of natural resources were available on the Black Mountain to meet the demands of developing industries, be they collieries or furnaces, as well as building materials for the housing stock that came with the industrial boom in the valley below and, of course, for constructing and maintaining the Black Mountain road itself.

CHAPTER 2

The Story of the Road

UNTIL RECENT ADVANCES in computer and telecoms technology, the means to communicate and trade with one another relied heavily on one's ability to travel. Transport has also been vital to the growth of the economy, assisting trade with others – locally and then further afield. Roads and bridges across rivers played a part in every area's development. This was true of the Black Mountain region as well.

A road over the Black Mountain was initially constructed to make it easier to transport coal to the lime quarries on the higher reaches of the mountain. This was just the beginning of opening up the wider area to development and making it far less remote. The road soon joined other turnpike roads, linking expanding villages in the Amman Valley.

According to several sources the 1819 Black Mountain road was constructed by a gentleman called John Jones of Brynbrain. (More information about him and his son John is to be found in the next chapter.) According to Enoch Rees, in his book *Hanes Brynaman* (1896), a tollgate was opened on the road in 1820. This road over the mountain has not been altered (just a few bends widened) or diverted in any way since then, and was an addition to an older turnpike road that traversed the mountain further to the west.

The road, now the A4069, is a great piece of engineering. It has a gradual incline from the southern / Brynaman side to the top of the mountain. There are no very steep gradients but it does have some spectacular bends as it twists, dips and climbs through the Brecon Beacons National Park. Many motoring journals describe it as a great driving road. 'Five of the most memorable miles you can drive in any country,' according to the television programme *Top Gear*.[1] With extensive views to the south, west and north, its highest point is 602 m (1,975 ft) above sea level. The drive down towards Gwynfe and Llangadog is steeper, and has a few more hairpin bends.

The road has two distinctive bends on each flank of the mountain. On the northern / Gwynfe side is the famed 180-degree bend known as Tro'r Gwcw (cuckoo corner). As children we were always told to make the sound of the bird as we drove around it. The origin of this name is a mystery. On the first Ordnance Survey drawing in 1826, the corner is called Tro Newydd (new corner). The other spectacular bend is on the southern / Brynaman side. This is called Tro'r Derlwyn (oak-grove corner) and turns abruptly west with a sheer drop down one side and the remains of old quarries on the other side.

John Jones Brynbrain probably had the vision for constructing this road because of the difficulty in transporting coal from his mines in Gwter Fawr (now Brynaman) up to the kilns and quarries on top of the mountain, and to communities on the other side of it.

The older turnpike road, towards the west, is now marked

as a footpath on maps. It is possible that this older road was built on an ancient track. Parts of it are still visible, with stones placed at the edges to stop travellers losing their way on what can be a bleak, misty landscape. Few are the landmarks to help guide you on your way, especially at dusk or in the dark. There are a number of sad stories about people who have perished on the mountain. One tells of Ann Williams of Rhiwddu who died 'in the great cold on the Black Mountain' on 9 April 1868.[2]

But why didn't John Jones just consider improving the existing turnpike road rather than constructing a new road in the 1810s? There are three possible reasons. Firstly, perhaps ruts made by carts over the years had made the first road difficult to upgrade. Secondly, there was probably a need for a road to be in use while the new one was being constructed and that could take quite a while. Thirdly, and the more likely reason, the need for a road constructed nearer to the newer quarries opening up on the mountain's summit.

An act of parliament was necessary for the construction of every mile of turnpike road – hence the term 'milestone' for old stone markers that can be seen at the side of old roadways throughout Britain today. There is one such milestone on the Black Mountain road on the Tro Derlwyn corner. Carved onto it is 'Llangadock 11 Miles'. This might not be the original milestone (although the milestone opposite the Ebenezer and Siloam chapels on the Banwen in Lower Brynaman is original and has a Grade II-listed status).

Early Roads

Hardly any records exist, before the late 18th century, of how man made the journey from north to south over the Black Mountain. There are traces of ancient footpaths and drovers' routes, but these were not recorded on early maps. The 'Black Mountain' is named as a 'feature' on these old maps.

Transport systems in the United Kingdom have always been closely regulated by statutory law. The law relating to highways has its origins in early medieval times. The Statute of Winchester 1285 was the first ever road act, and it decreed that bushes and undergrowth should be cleared on each side of a highway in the interests of safety. After this there were various piecemeal measures until the Highways Act of 1555, which was the foundation of highway law for nearly three centuries.[3] This act was passed in response to complaints by travellers about the state of the roads, and it made roads the responsibility of parish councils to maintain. Surveyors were appointed, and they had to find men able to give up six days of free labour to work on the roads (and this practice existed from 1689 until 1835). In the early 18th century the work was often allocated to local craftsmen such as carpenters, masons and bricklayers. However, with increasing traffic on roads, some were often impassable and not improvable by locals, so had to be transferred to the turnpike trusts for maintenance.[4]

Maps

Maps prior to the 19th century show that there were no roads or tracks surrounding the River Amman (called 'Amon' on 18th-century maps), south of the Black Mountain, except for a ford near where Glanaman is now. These early maps only show major routes in Wales, and those in the Black Mountain area go around it, from Llangadog towards Llandybie and Llandeilo on the western side.

The earliest map which showed Wales as a region separate from England, *Cambriae Typus*, was completed by the time of the death of its creator, Humphrey Llwyd (Lhuyd), in 1568. What is interesting about this map, although mainly in Latin, is that it has several Welsh spellings, for example: L. Gadoc for Llangadog. Humphrey Llwyd was a Welsh speaker and had been educated at Oxford University. His map shows major mountain ranges, rivers and principal towns, but not roads. A contemporary of Humphrey Llwyd was Christopher Saxton. His famous map of Radnor, Brecknock, Cardigan and Carmarthen in 1578 shows roads around Llangadog and Llanddeusant to the north of the Black Mountain, and Llandybie to the west, but no connecting route over the mountain from north to south. The Black Mountain is clearly depicted on Saxton's map of *Caermarden* (Carmarthenshire). This was the first important map showing the counties during the reign of Elizabeth I. The first published atlas relating specifically to Wales and depicting all of the counties of Wales, *The Principality of Wales Exactly Described* (1718) by Thomas Taylor, shows roads and rivers to the north and west of the Black Mountain but, again, nothing crossing from Llangadog directly south to the River Amman.[5]

John Ogilvy published the first ever British road atlas, *Britannia*, in 1675. This was radically different, as the most important features of the landscape recorded were the roads. His 'strip maps' followed the route of roads and became very popular, evidence of the increasing importance of

29

travel in social, political and early industrial development. His maps continued to be produced for much of the 18th century. Several of his routes begin or end in Wales and a few are set entirely in Wales. As the present road over the mountain was not constructed until the 19th century, the Black Mountain is just named and shows no track going over it. It was not until 1830, when the Ordnance Survey produced what is now called the 'Old Series Maps', that a road going from north to south from Llangadog to Gwaun-Cae-Gurwen, through Gwter Fawr (now Brynaman) is recorded on a map. This 1830 map shows both the old turnpike road going past Bryn Uchaf farm, as well as the new road constructed by John Jones Brynbrain going past Craig y Derlwyn.[6]

Drovers' routes crossed the Carmarthenshire countryside in all directions and one is known to have crossed over the Black Mountain above Ystradgynlais and Cwmtwrch, and formed part of an ancient route by which cattle were driven from Glamorgan to the Tywi Valley.[7] No records exist of which track they followed over the mountain. However, the numerous local names which include 'pedol' (meaning animal shoe), such as Cwm Pedol on the hills to the north of Brynaman, would suggest the route was near there. It is generally thought that the Llanddeusant area on the northern side of the Black Mountain was one of the principal drovers' calling places, with cattle and sheep being driven from the Gower Peninsula as well to sales at Brecon fair. Welsh butter was transported in carts from Pembroke to Merthyr to be sold. Driving cattle and other stock along these old tracks came to an end as better roads were constructed by the turnpike trusts. A way of life was changing; ancient rural fairs declined as markets were established near to new railway towns. Llangadog had an annual fair dating back to the 13th century and kept its market which was used by drovers.

Turnpike Roads and Tollhouses

Turnpike roads were one of the crucial innovations which spurred the growth of the Industrial Revolution. In 1663, parliament passed the first Turnpike Act authorizing a toll or payment for the use of a road. Later, these turnpike acts set up trusts with powers to collect tolls from anyone using turnpike roads, with the income accrued going towards repairing and improving roads.

However, it wasn't until the 1720s that turnpike trusts became more widespread. 'Turnpike mania' followed between 1751 and 1772, when turnpike trusts were established to cover more than 11,500 miles of road in England and Wales. By 1838, 942 acts had set up new turnpike trusts, resulting in approximately 22,000 miles of turnpike road. However, not all roads were turnpike, and other roads and lanes constructed were the responsibility of the local parish and were toll free. Turnpike roads made up a fifth of the entire road network.[8] Constructing turnpike roads declined with the coming of the railways.[9] The Local Government Act of 1888 gave responsibility for maintaining main roads to county councils and county borough councils.[10] Although tollgates were perceived as an impediment to free trade as the Industrial Revolution advanced, the legacy of the turnpike trust system is a network of roads that still forms the framework of the British road system to this day.

In 1779, in the Black Mountain area, the Llangadock and Llandovery Turnpike Trust was established, and was responsible for turnpike roads in the area, as well as constructing the very first road over the Black Mountain which ran from the Towy Valley near Llangadog to Cwmaman. The motive for the construction of this road was to reach the limekilns on the slopes of the mountain. This lime was on the edge of a coalfield, and a link was needed between the Towy and Amman valleys via the quarries on top of the Black Mountain.

The Llangadock and Llandovery Turnpike Trust Minutes for 8 July 1779 records constructing a section of road 'from the back parts of Cwmllwyd south towards Amman'. This earliest road over the mountain was called Bryn Road (it started in Brynaman, joining the Llangadog road to a gate at Cwmcoy, north-west of Gwynfe).[11] This Llangadog to Brynaman old turnpike can be found about a mile to the west of the present A4069, and, as noted, is marked as a footpath on today's maps. This old turnpike road still exists, with its side walls and gravel surface visible in parts. You can follow its path for almost its entire length across the mountain, apart from the last mile on the Brynaman side where the reed bogs have taken over. Walking along its length, it's surprising how wide this original road was, probably so that two carts could pass each other without difficulty. Wagon drivers or the traveller must have been grateful for the boundary sides as a guide in the dark. On the route you pass an archaeological site called 'Carn Pen y Clogau', an ancient enclosure and cairn.

As well as tollgates on the main turnpike roads, 'side-bars' were set up on smaller roads to catch any traffic trying to avoid the main routes. Not every road had a tollhouse built specifically to collect tolls, but the trusts often used 'toll farmers' to collect payments.[12] The Llandovery and Llangadock Turnpike Trust had 41 miles of road and 13 gates to supervise. This works out at a tollgate every three miles or so. The turnpike trusts themselves fixed the charges and decided how many tollgates should be built.[13]

Tolls made it very expensive for people to transport lime to market. Lime was a soil improver, so farmers might use as much as four tons of lime on an acre of land each year. Farmers who did not have easy access locally to lime had to travel long distances to get it. So lime from the Black Mountain area was transported as far away as Aberaeron on the Cardiganshire coast, a journey which could take two or three days. The number of tolls on such a journey must have been a huge drain on farmers' finances. If a return journey wasn't made within 24 hours, the tolls would be charged again. Farmers, therefore, would queue up with their carts at the tollgates early in the morning, trying to reduce costs by completing their journeys in a day.

A former tollgate building (which is now a dwelling) can still be seen at the bottom of the Black Mountain on the northern / Gwynfe side, near the cattle-grid. However, the location of the first tollgate or tollhouse on the southern / Brynaman side is less clear. As noted, Enoch Rees says that the latter was 'established' in 1820 and describes it as being located in the 'higher' house of a row of three houses near to where 'the Company' had its stables. This would probably have been near the River Amman. The Ordnance Survey Old Series Map, published 1830, places a tollgate near the River Amman where the railway station was later positioned. However, another possibility could be the small building erected along the wall surrounding Gibea cemetery (opposite today's Mountain Heritage Centre / old school, and near the roundabout which is the start of the mountain road now). This building's front elevation has been altered, as it served as a chemist for many years and had a large window. This tollhouse would have preceded Gibea Chapel, which was built in 1856. Needing to stand alone, potentially, the tollhouse is unlikely to have been in the row of three houses Enoch Rees suggests. The 1891 census seems to confirm this small building in the cemetery's boundary wall as the tollhouse. It is listed as the 'Old Gate House'.

It has been documented that there were at least six toll structures of some sort on the road between Llangadog and Brynaman. Two tollhouses' remains survive, and only two out of the 13 milestones.

Rebecca Riots

When looking at the history of turnpike roads, the Rebecca Riots have to be mentioned as Carmarthenshire was one of the main areas of unrest. The Rebecca Riots were a series of protests in rural parts of Wales between 1839 and 1843 and are usually remembered as attacks on tollgates. But, they were also protests about the economic hardships of the time and the relationship between farmers and landlords, and the payment of tithes to the Established Church.

In the main, tenant farmers attacked tollgates, opposing payments charged to use the roads. They called themselves 'Rebecca and her daughters'. The rioters often included one or more 'Rebecca' figures dressed up and disguised in women's clothes. The name Rebecca came from a biblical verse, Genesis 24:60: 'And they blessed Rebekah, and said unto her, Thou *art* our sister, be thou *the mother* of thousands of millions, and let thy seed possess the gate of those which hate them.' People were very knowledgeable about the Bible in those days as they attended chapel frequently, so the significance of the name would not have been lost on them.

In the first half of the 19th century agricultural communities suffered from bad weather which resulted in poor harvests and fluctuating market values for their produce. With reduced incomes and increased rents, further rates and tolls made life very difficult. There were a dozen tollgates into the market town of Carmarthen, meaning that it felt like a fortress. Carmarthenshire was experiencing a difficult period of transition and a depression in the years prior to 1843. The first riot was in the summer of 1839, with riots peaking in number during the winter of 1842. By late 1843 the riots had subsided as the government increased the number of troops in the area. In 1844, an act was passed to control the powers of turnpike trusts.[14]

Details are recorded of riots in Carmarthen and on the Gwynfe / Llangadog side of the mountain. No riots specific to the Gwter Fawr / Brynaman side of the mountain have come to light in my research. This could be because it was developing as an industrial rather than agricultural area, and was therefore not as dependent on using the roads to obtain lime for soil improvement and carrying goods and animals to market.

There were riots near Llandybie, which was another area for lime quarries. In Llangadog, in September 1843, three gates were attacked during one night. The closest the rioters came to the road which traverses over the Black Mountain was the tollgate known as Pontarllechau. This is on the road to Llangadog, a few miles north of Gwynfe. In 1843, special constables were 'compelled to destroy the gate and tollhouse' after rioting took place. Why the tollhouse near the cattle-grid in Gwynfe, mentioned earlier, was not attacked is surprising. Perhaps it was built after the period of the riots or perhaps special constables were on guard there at all times.

There are reports of secret meetings held in the hills during the winter of 1843. These meetings were to discuss grievances and the actions that those attending could take, be they passive petitions or active rioting. Twelve hundred attended a meeting in Cefn Coed near Llangadog and there was another meeting held at Bryn Cwmllynfell on the southern slopes of the Black Mountain on 22 September 1843. This meeting addressed issues such as the system of government and administration which was felt to be outdated, the tithes, poor law, inadequacies of the magistrates, high rents and the Corn Laws. A distinguished public figure, Franklin Lewis JP, was recorded as maintaining that the rioters' cause was just.[15]

As a consequence of the Rebecca Riots, a commission was appointed in 1844 to investigate and report on the turnpike trusts in south Wales. It recommended changes to the turnpike system, stating that tolls should be made uniform across the country: sixpence for a horse-drawn cart, four pence for a horse and cart, and one and a half pence for a horse (previously a trust could decide its own charges). A superintendent of roads should be appointed by the government and reside in south Wales. This report,

The Commission of Inquiry for South Wales, resulted in the eventual abolition of the trusts and the creation instead of the Carmarthenshire County Roads Board in 1845 to supervise road systems.

Carmarthenshire County Roads Board

The Carmarthenshire County Roads Board was in operation for 44 years. Much of its early work was in removing the excessive tollgates. Carmarthenshire was the largest county in Wales between 1845 and 1889, and had the greatest mileage of roads to maintain.

The Board established a sub-board, the Llandovery District Board, and this was responsible for the routes over the Black Mountain. The tolls didn't all stop immediately but their regulation meant that there was no repeat of rioting. Tollgates were now to be set seven miles apart, and local farm produce was to be exempt, with a surveyor overseeing movement.

Agricultural prosperity returned after the riots. There was increased demand and a market for produce as a result of the rapidly growing industrial areas. The coming of the railways also contributed to the end of turnpike roads and trusts, and facilitated migration from rural areas to the growing industrial areas. Rural poverty declined, people were on the move, and the demand for rural produce, trade, skills in carpentry, masonry and labour in general, grew.

When the Carmarthenshire County Roads Board came to an end in 1889, and Carmarthenshire County Council took over, the roads were regarded as being in excellent order and condition.

Financing the 1819 road over the Black Mountain

A description of the Black Mountain road, dated 1840, in a petition to parliament says that '20 miles of this road [is] for the transfer of lime, the greatest part of which runs over a high and exposed mountain, for the repair of which a large sum has annually been expended by the Trust'.[16]

The initiative for applying for an act to construct a road depended on the public or private interests of individuals. Other factors, such as the nature of the soil, the gradient of the terrain, whether any local labour was available, influenced the decision on whether it was possible to build a road. It was getting access to the quarries on the summit that influenced the need for a better road over the Black Mountain, as well as local entrepreneurs' business interests.

Notices published in newspapers in the early 1810s say that this new road over the Black Mountain was a part of the Llangadock and Llandovery Turnpike Trust. At first, this turnpike trust built and repaired the old turnpike road up as far as the Brest Cwm Llwyd limekilns on the northern slopes, but as limestone quarrying moved eastwards, a new road was needed. The Llangadock and Llandovery Turnpike Trust initially had no interest in extending the 'moorland track' beyond the kilns. In 1799 the villagers of Gwynfe were expected to maintain the road from Gwynfe to the gate at Rhiwddu Farm, with the Trust then responsible for the remainder as far as the kilns at Brest Cwm Llwyd.[17]

The history of turnpike trusts shows that their members were usually made up of landowners and businessmen. Tenant and yeoman farmers, aristocracy and even clergy were often investors too. The trusts were regarded as profitable investments at the time, as better maintained roads enhanced an area's competitive position for wider markets. Trusts were seen as a secure investment with good returns, and viewed as less risky than investing in the other fast growing industries and commerce of the time. Trusts would mortgage tolls based on the expected income received from the tollgates – as a means of borrowing funds to raise capital for improvements and repairs. Bonds were secured on the tolls, with the trustees adding their personal security for any loans. Farmers and gentry would appear to be the most important sources of income for turnpike trusts, whereas merchants, manufacturers and industrialists would lend their 'support' to turnpike trusts. But, their 'financial contributions do not seem to have been always commensurate with their concerns'.[18]

It is interesting to note that other men had tried to construct the new road over the Black Mountain, namely a Richard Bevan from Neath who, in 1780, commenced working on a road to connect Felindre, near Llangadog, with the Amman Valley, but could not get full payment from trustees, so the venture was abandoned. In 1784 work was carried out by a Richard Williams to build 1,350 yards of road. Then, a John Nethanial built a further one mile – this stretch of road originated in the Amman Valley but it isn't clear in which direction it went.[19]

The Llangadock and Llandovery Turnpike Trust had first started showing an interest in constructing a new road over the mountain in 1812, and permission was granted in a 1813 Act for a new road to go over the mountain all the way to the Glamorgan county boundary.[20]

The road was later extended to Gwaun-Cae-Gurwen. Exact dates for this differ, ranging from 1824 to 1830. A coloured, hand-drawn plan at Glamorgan Archives, dated 1830, by John Williams, shows the mountain road ending at the bridge crossing the River Amman, and a proposed plan for a road to Gwaun-Cae-Gurwen linking it to the 'Mountain Gate' on the Neath to Llandeilo turnpike road. This was to replace an older road or track leading to the colliery at Gwter Fawr, described as being 'exceedingly steep and boggy'.[21] There is also another proposed road on this 1830 map, linking the mountain road from the Tro Derlwyn corner straight across to Garnant, but this doesn't seem to have been constructed. In fact, John Jones himself didn't want to extend the road further than his coal mine in Gwter Fawr (present-day Lower Brynaman) but, because of the demands of others, mainly men from Gwynfe who wanted to extend access to potential markets, he eventually accepted its extension towards Gwaun-Cae-Gurwen.[22]

As already noted, a tollhouse was built in Brynaman in 1820 and only turnpike trusts could collect road tolls. John Jones's will suggests that his shares in the Llangadock and Llandovery Turnpike Trust were bequeathed to his daughter Jane Rowland. As a trustee, with coal from his mines being transported on the road, he would have had a say in the charges set.

Later in the century, in 1878, another possible source of financial assistance to build roads came from the Exchequer Bill Loan Commission which was authorised to issue £1,750,000 as loans to further help public works in order to 'afford employment for the labouring classes and communities'. However, trustees were often required to give their personal bonds too and, because of the Commission's strict conditions, their assistance was only sought when no other source of finance could be found. This was a possible way for such a big project to be financed at the time.

The National Library of Wales has documents relating to the Llangadock and Llandovery Turnpike Trust and the Carmarthen County Roads Board. One, dated 24 March 1848, lists the Black Mountain road in its accounts for that quarter of that year. This road would appear to be the most costly for the Trust, but it does attribute the high cost of repairs to floods in the previous December at Sawdde Bridge near Llangadog. The length of the road listed as the Black Mountain road is 12 miles. If it started near Sawdde Bridge, then it would confirm that the Black Mountain road ended at the bridge on the River Amman in Gwter Fawr (now Brynaman), near John Jones's coal mine. In October 1848 there is a record in the Minutes which shows that John Jones, his son, was present, as he is listed when the state of the road from Llangadog over the Black Mountain was discussed (the matter was to be referred to the newly established Llandovery District Board).[23]

How was the road built?

As no actual records exist, the following is conjecture. In order to try and answer some questions, suggestions are made from research into what techniques were available at the time.

Who decided on the route of the road?

According to the *Amman Valley Chronicle*, 4 September 1919, John Jones Senior 'engineered the pass and supervised operations'. As for deciding on the new road's route, the quarries were extending higher up the mountain than the earlier workings, therefore the original turnpike road was no longer as easily accessible to these businesses. The new road was located about a mile from the existing road, and closer to the new quarries at the summit.

An oral account, from the 1930s, suggests how the route of the road was decided upon. The builder of the road attached a cart to a donkey and then let it loose to see how it got up the mountain, and this is the route that the road followed. My father often heard this story as a boy when living on Caedraw, a smallholding on the edge of the mountain in Rhosaman.

What materials were used?

Rocks found on the mountain were used. It's unlikely that materials came from much further away as the road network at the time was poor, the area remote, and that would have greatly added to the cost. Looking at the older turnpike road, which is now a footpath over the mountain, the remains of the foundations are still evident, showing that local stone found scattered on the mountain was used.

Our modern tarred roads are the result of work by two Scottish engineers, Thomas Telford and John McAdam, contemporaries of John Jones Brynbrain. Thomas Telford (1757–1834) designed the system of raising the foundations of a road in the centre to drain water from the surface. He improved the method of building roads with broken stone by analysing stone thickness, road traffic, road alignment and gradients.

John McAdam (1756–1836) invented a new process for

building roads: a smooth hard surface on a firm base of larger stones, using broken stones laid in tight patterns and covered with small stones to create a hard surface. McAdam discovered that the best stone or gravel for road surfacing had to be broken or crushed, and then graded to a constant size of chippings which would be more durable than a soil-based track, laid to a total thickness of between eight and twelve inches.

In 1819 McAdam was putting forward proposals to parliamentary enquiries noting that roads needed to be raised above the surrounding ground and constructed from layered rocks and gravel. McAdam had been appointed surveyor to the Bristol Turnpike Trust in 1816. He made their roads slightly convex, with a camber which meant water drained off easily and did not damage the foundations. This was the greatest advancement in road design since the Romans and became known as 'macadamisation' or 'macadam'.[24] John Jones may have read about this in the newspapers and it may have influenced the design of the Black Mountain road. The McAdam method spread very quickly across the world. The first McAdam road in North America, the National Road, was completed in the 1830s and most of the main roads in Europe were subject to the McAdam process by the end of the 19th century. McAdam roads were the forerunners of the bitumen-based binding that was to become tarmacadam. The word tarmacadam was shortened to the now familiar tarmac. McAdam was made Surveyor-General of Metropolitan Roads in 1820.

It is interesting to note here that his efficient road building and management work revealed the corruption and abuse of some unscrupulous turnpike trusts. They were responsible for the structural work and repairs of their roads and bridges, and appointed a surveyor as a salaried officer. In 1825, a report submitted to Parliament by John McAdam criticised these surveyors, stating that the greater part of the problems with road systems was down to them. McAdam only commented on turnpike trust roads in England (over a period of 20 years) but his influence was national.

According to letters held at Carmarthen Archives, it would appear that John McAdam visited Wales, as there are letters sent by him from Tenby and Narberth showing his dealings with the Carmarthen Turnpike Trust.[25] In fact, on 28 June 1836, he billed a Mr J. Stacey of Carmarthen for his monthly allowance: 'Mr Hale will wait upon you to receive the usual monthly allowance,' in a letter sent from Tenby. The correspondence between the two men is mainly regarding roads in the St Clears area and gives an estimate for the cost of a tollhouse and gate as £50 and £70 respectively. McAdam appears to have been working for the Carmarthen Turnpike Trust for a number of years. John Louden McAdam died in 1836 but his sons carried on the work and perhaps continued to use his name on all official letters and documents.[26] One interesting letter, dated 16 July 1842, illustrates unhappiness with surveyors: 'Our family have long since agreed never to recommend a surveyor... we adopt this course in consequence of having been often disappointed in their conduct.'

Who were the workers employed to construct and maintain the road?

They were all probably local men, farmers, perhaps

some miners who worked for John Jones. Later, when the Carmarthenshire County Roads Board took over responsibility for its upkeep and others, permanent labour was employed to maintain roads. In 1845 the Llandovery District Board employed 37 men, but this dropped to 13 by the 1880s. Men were paid fortnightly and, in an area of mostly small-holding farmers, the road-mending job was attractive for its regular work and income and not much harder or more exposed to the elements than farming. These men, although given protective clothing to wear, had to provide their own equipment, such as a wheelbarrow, pickaxe, spade, shovel, rake, scraper and stone hammer.[27] In 1811 McAdam, in one of his reports, gave a list of equipment needed to repair the turnpike roads as 'picks, sledge hammers, small hammers... wheelbarrows... iron rakes'. He even stipulated that the hammer should be 15 inches long, with the head only half-an-inch in size. The rakes used should only be ten inches long, with 'short teeth not to exceed an inch and a half in length'.[28] An interesting piece of information to add here is that McAdam regarded women as being more suitable to the task of breaking up stone. He writes, 'a woman sitting will break more stone for a road than two strong laborers on their feet with long hammers, in a given time'.[29] It is not known if women were employed in the construction of the Black Mountain road. At the Carmarthen Turnpike Trust only the names of men are shown on payment slips.[30]

How long did it take to construct the road?

Planning the road took a few years. As noted earlier, in *The Cambrian*, 26 September 1812, a notice was placed requesting permission to build a road over the Black Mountain from the existing limekilns 'making the road… as far as the confines of the counties of Carmarthen and Glamorgan', that is to the River Amman in Brynaman where the two counties meet. Sources state that it had been constructed by 1819, and Enoch Rees notes in his book that a tollgate was opened in 1820. Turnpike roads were built per mile. There are approximately eight miles from Upper Brynaman to Gwynfe. The terrain and steepness of the road, and getting men and equipment up the mountain, all played a factor in the time it took to construct, as well as the weather conditions. It's unlikely that any work was carried out over the severe winter months or wet springs. Therefore, from planning to completion, it took approximately seven years – from 1813 to 1820, when the tollgate opened.

According to newspaper reports, John Jones, the son, was involved in on-going disputes about the maintenance of the road decades after it was completed and the turnpike trusts abolished. For example, an article in *The Welshman*, dated 6 November 1857, says:

> John Jones Esqr. of Brynbrain, charged the Surveyor of the High-ways, for the District of Llangadog, with non-repair of a Highway near Gwinfe. Mr Jones, appeared for the complainant, and Mr Bishop, for the defendant, who disputed the liability of the Hamlet to repair the road in dispute, in consequence of which the Justices ordered an indictment to be preferred at the next Assizes, for the non-repair of the Highway.

How much did it cost to construct the road?

As noted, no records exist about the financing or construction of this road. However, such information exists for other roads in the area, therefore it is possible to give some indication of costs. For example, Mr John Bowen, a surveyor to the clerk of the Llandovery to Llangadock Main Trust, for 17 August 1814, writes 'for repairing the whole of the Turnpike road stone and gravel the sum of £20 to fill the track breaks... for the upkeep and constant repair £15 per mile'.[31]

Cost for labourers:

- breaking stone – 2 shillings and 18 pence for 53 yards
- 2 days' work building a wall – 5 shillings
- 1 day's work for putting up a milestone – 1 shilling
- 46 days of carting – 6 shillings and 16 pence[32]

According to the Turnpike Act 1784, the road leading to the 'town of Llangadock and Sawdde Bridge are in a ruinous condition, narrow and incommodious for travellers and in some places impassable for carriages'.[33] No such reports have been found about the Black Mountain road constructed several decades later.

The Centenary of the Road in 1919

An article in the *Cambria Daily Leader*, 19 April 1919, was entitled 'Centenary of a Road'. The author described John Jones Brynbrain, Cwmllynfell, as 'The Maker of the Pass... planning and surveying were his chief hobbies and the pioneer of all great improvements'. The article adds, 'present day [1919] expert Surveyors' who had inspected

47

the road declared it a 'clever engineering attainment and hard to improve upon'.

The article noted that the road had been constructed right down to the River Amman and that John Jones 'took it upon himself to construct a bridge across the river'. When the road was constructed he apparently levelled up what was before a deep 'thickety ravine'. This appears to refer to the point where the road crosses the river at the top of Station Road just below Gibea Chapel.

John Jones is also credited with building the bridge at the bottom of Station Road. This bridge, near today's rugby club, was known as 'Pont y Ffarmers', also as 'Pont Pwll y Cwar' and was built in 1819 by John Jones Brynbrain[34] according to an article written in 1913 in the *Amman Valley Chronicle*. 'Brynaman Notes' says that the old bridge, 'called Pont y Ffarmers changed little in its structure since first built'.

As noted, although John Jones, at first, resisted extending the Black Mountain road beyond the bridge towards Gwaun-Cae-Gurwen, as the market for coal grew it was inevitable that the road needed to be connected to other turnpike roads in the Amman Valley. According to Enoch Rees, donkeys were originally used to carry coal to Glanaman, and the road that went from there to Llandeilo had been in existence since 1817. Therefore, connecting to other turnpike roads was an attractive proposition as more coal mines and quarries opened for production.

South Wales had a better system of roads than most other areas. An extract from *Llais Llafur* [Labour voice] newspaper, 3 May 1919, says:

Parents of many people now living remember quite well this road being built, the very excellent feat of building a road over the Black Mountain was engineered by John Jones of Brynbrain, and this remains a lasting monument to the memory of one who must have been a very clever man. When we bear in mind that the Black Mountain reaches a height of 2,000 feet above sea level and the road runs right across its brow, the magnitude of the work can be partly realised.

Despite indecision and neglect in most areas, the fate of the turnpike roads after the coming of the railways in south Wales was the exception, with an 'effective framework of administration which was the consequence of the Rebecca Riots' and an attempt to avoid further protests.[35] Therefore, the Black Mountain road, with its unique, distinctive large boulders as road markings[36], benefited and has been maintained ever since.

CHAPTER 3

John Jones Brynbrain – Father and Son

JOHN JONES SENIOR of Brynbrain is credited with opening several coal mines, being an important player in the construction of the road over the Black Mountain, the bridges that cross the River Amman, as well as the road linking Cwmllynfell to Brynaman. His son John Jones is known to have built Brynaman House in 1838/9 and this still stands on Station Road in Brynaman. John Jones, the son, was also instrumental in bringing the railway to the village. Details about these two men are scarce and, as noted, they often get confused and thought of as one man. Even their signatures, as seen on wills, church records and legal documents, are very similar.

John Jones Senior (1759–1835)

John Jones Senior was described in his will as 'John Jones the Elder, Brynbrain, Gentleman'[1], probably as a way of distinguishing himself from his son. However, on his gravestone he is 'Mr John Jones'. The title of 'Mr' on a gravestone is unusual, with titles such as Reverend or Doctor only used normally.

He lived all his life on the family farm of Brynbrain in the hamlet of Cefnbrynbrain near Brynaman. Early 19th-century maps of this area show a remote and thinly populated expanse with only a few scattered farms and cottages. The farm was located where several footpaths met, and it could have been an important place for employment in pre-industrial times. Looking at the farm today, the terrain appears fertile and well drained, with large trees that give it a more cultivated appearance compared to the mountain lands that surround it. Notable features of the farm are the large, thick, dry-stone walls which are not that common in this neck of the woods.

It was the birthplace of John Jones Senior, but no member of the Jones family live on the farm these days. The Jones family owned the farm for generations up until the late 1880s. John Jones Senior's father was known as Evan John of Brynbrain (the Jones surname only started to be used in the next generation). Evan John was born in 1726 on the then 60-acre farm, but Evan was a tailor by trade. Evan and his wife Elisabeth were members of Cwmllynfell's chapel. However, their first two children, including John, were baptised at Ystradgynlais Parish Church, as Cwmllynfell's 'meeting house', as it was then known, had yet to be granted permission for registering births. John was born on 26 November 1759 and baptised on 1 December. He was the eldest of four children.

John's grandmother, Jennett Awbrey (died 1768) and originally from Ystradgynlais, married a John Evan in the 1720s. She came from a wealthy family in Ystradgynlais and their ancestry goes back to the Tudors. Queen Elizabeth I granted lands in Breconshire to a Dr William Aubrey (there is interchangeable spelling). Another member of the Aubrey family later acquired the Ynyscedwyn Estate in Ystradgynlais through marriage to the Franklin family.[2] As with so many landed families, estates were added to through marriage and inheritance, sometimes through the female line if sons died without issue. The Awbrey family and estate became a casualty of declining industry in the Swansea Valley, with Ynyscedwyn House eventually being demolished in 1997.

As for her grandson's education, perhaps Jennett would have passed on what education she had received coming from a wealthy family. At the time of his boyhood, 'circulating schools' were operating in Cwmllynfell. These schools offered, through the medium of Welsh, religious instruction and it can be assumed that the Jones family took advantage of this (the first National School in Cwmllynfell was not established until 1849/50). John Jones Senior must have had some formal education, as his documents at the chapel he attended were all written in English.

Not much is known of John Jones Senior's early life but it can be assumed that the family were fairly wealthy. The farm appears prosperous enough to have a large house built in 1795, with two-storey outhouses added in 1806. A small, simple plaque is set into one building, with the inscription 'built by John Jones' and the date. John, though, did not own the farm. It was owned by his sister, Mary. However, he lived there all his life, sharing the farm with his growing family and sister.

Although John Jones built and bought new farms during his lifetime, he never moved to live in any of them. He owned several farms at the start of the 19th century in Cwmllynfell,

Gwaun-Cae-Gurwen and as far as Neath. One of his biggest purchases was Hendreforgan Farm, Llangiwg, also known as Bryndillis Gwylfa, which he bought in 1813. The farm at the time had about 98 acres of land and was located on the south-west side of the River Llynfell near Cwmllynfell. Other properties and land he is known to have owned or leased in the Gwter Fawr / Brynamam and Cwmllynfell areas were Penal Farm, Blaencwmteg cottage and croft, Cefn Garth, Lleti'r Garth, Bryn Llefrith, Yniswen Farm, Cilybebyll, Bryn Caws, Derlwyn and Gellynydd. How he came to own so many farms is unclear but it would seem that, as his businesses grew in profitability, he bought the farms because he was aware of their land's potential mineral value. Some land, of course, he would have inherited as the eldest son, but most of the land was bought as an investment. He would have known of industrial developments happening elsewhere; perhaps recognised the business potential the geology of the area had to offer. All of these farms were later passed on to his sons, illustrating that John Jones Brynbrain was indeed a wealthy individual at the time of his death.

He lived in Brynbrain with his wife Jane and their four sons, Evan, John, Owen and Jonah, and two daughters, one named Angharad who later was married to a Mr Watkins who owned one of the first shops in Brynaman. Another daughter, Jane, married twice; both men were ministers at Cwmllynfell Chapel, the Rev. Rowland and the Rev. Rhys Pryse (more about the Rev. Pryse in Chapter 4).

John, the second eldest son, had a role in John Jones Senior's enterprises in developing industry and bringing prosperity to Brynaman. According to John Jones Senior's will, his son John inherited Blaencwmteg Farm and Gwter

Fawr Colliery. Two other sons, Owen and Evan, managed farms built or bought by John Jones Senior. Jonah, the youngest son (his twin having died young) and a bachelor into his forties, inherited Gorsto Farm. The eldest son, Evan, was granted the mineral rights to Hendreforgan Farm. Hendreforgan Colliery was located near the farm on the River Llynfell. Evan appeared to be more interested in following a vocation as a farmer rather than involving himself with coal mining.

A local newspaper headline, 'Pioneer of Brynaman', in 1824, noted that a John Jones also made money from selling wood, and buying farms on the proceeds. However, this may have been one of the son's early business ventures.[3] John Jones Senior built at least two farms. One was a 167-acre farm, Bryn Llefrith in Cwmllynfell. This farm disappeared when opencast mining came to the area. However, a full description of this farm as it was in 1807 exists in a publication by the Historic Farm Buildings Group.[4] At the time Bryn Llefrith was farmed by a Henry Jones, who could have been a family member. The 1871 census says that Henry Jones had been born in 1792 and lived on the farm as a bailiff.

Another farm, Bryn Caws, built by John Jones Senior, in 1812, is located near Neath and was farmed by his son Owen. Owen Jones went on to become a pillar of his community, building a chapel on his land and, according to an obituary written at the time of his death, in 1877, he was 'the kindest of men'.[5] This farm had been bequeathed to Owen in his father's will, along with a property called Tir y Mill or Dirllwyn in Cadoxton parish near Neath.

John Jones Senior started buying coal mines in the

early part of the 19th century, firstly a small mine called Blaengurwen Colliery, Rhosaman, in 1802. In 1810 he opened Big Vein at Gwter Fawr (present-day Brynaman). By 1812 he took over the Hendreforgan Colliery at Cwmllynfell, but sold it on later. As noted already, he made money by selling coal to the limestone quarries on top of the Black Mountain, and owned a small quarry himself. In 1819 he opened Lefel yr Office and Gwter Fawr collieries, located where Lower Brynaman is now.

What kind of a man was John Jones Senior? Much like many of his contemporaries, he was Welsh in 'speech and committed Nonconformists, stalwarts of local chapels who concerned themselves with the religious and cultural life of the area'.[6] In the book *Hanes Eglwys Cwmllynfell*, there are a few snippets of information about John Jones. He served as a deacon and was the chapel's secretary for many years up until his death in 1835. He is described as a scholarly person (although no mention is made of his actual education) and a prominent person in the community. He kept very detailed financial accounts of the chapel's business as its secretary and treasurer. There follows a transcribed section of a John Jones entry in the chapel book: 'July the 10th 1813. We whose names are here under subscribed do herby promise to pay... the sum opposite our names ... towards widening and repairing the Meeting House (Cwmllynfell) ... by four equal instalments'.[7] These payments varied from five shillings to £20, and 302 subscriber names are recorded, amounting to £391 4s. 2d. John Jones probably paid one of the larger amounts, as he was a deacon, gentleman farmer and businessman in the area.

The original chapel books are now stored at the National

Archives and are no longer available to view physically but have been digitalised. Interestingly, all of his entries were written in English, whereas subsequent records by others are all in Welsh. He was the first person to be elected as chapel secretary on a permanent basis; previously chapel secretaries were appointed annually. He transferred the ownership of one of his properties, Yniswen Farm, to the chapel in 1813. The rental income from the farm contributed towards the salary of the chapel minister. John Jones was a valued member of the chapel in every sense.

John Jones is also described as a gentleman. He expected his daughters to marry well, but apparently objected when one fell in love with a new preacher who lodged with them on the farm. Although he respected ministers for their religious leadership, these men were not financially well off and came generally from working-class backgrounds. Daughter Jane was sent to live with her brother Owen in Ystradgynlais. However, she eventually married her preacher, a Rev. Rowland, and they went to live at Gorsto Farm which was owned by her father. The Rev. Rowland was the minister at Cwmllynfell Chapel from 1822 until his death to 1834. Jane later married the next minister, the Rev. Rhys Pryse.

John Jones is mentioned in the newspaper *Tarian y Gweithiwr* [Worker's shield], dated 26 December 1889. The article discusses Cwmllynfell Chapel and tells how John Jones was the 'first to wear braces' despite there being a number of 'swells' in the congregation. He evidently had the means and inclination to dress the part of a gentleman.

The inscription on John Jones's grave makes for interesting reading: 'Here lie the remains of Mr John

Jones of Brynbrain who died on 15 May in 1835, 76 years in age. He was an affectionate husband, a kind father and good neighbour. He lived beloved and died lamented.' The inscription, now fading away, is written in English, followed by a biblical verse written in Welsh. There is also a plaque inside the foyer of the present chapel, giving details of his birth and death, with 'In the memory of Mr John Jones Brynbrain'. An old *Western Mail* article, from 1903, about early mine owners says 'they belonged to the old school of colliery proprietors who came into daily contact with their men, living and going to Church with the men in their communities'. This would be true of John Jones as well.

John Jones's gravestone is in a derelict, almost forgotten cemetery in Cwmllynfell, near the site of the first chapel on the banks of the River Llynfell. His gravestone stands out as it has been placed against the cemetery wall in a more prominent position facing inwards when the old chapel was extended in 1861. His grave, along with his son-in-law, the Rev. Rhys Pryse, were originally close to the first building.

John Jones Senior contributed much to the early success of the district. As a result of his endeavours, there were many successful coal mines along the valley during the early 19th century and, as the coal industry grew, more and more people were drawn to the area.

John Jones Junior (1795–1871)

It was John Jones's second son, not his first, who continued with the father's coal mining business. His other sons appear to have been more interested in farming. John showed an interest in the growing coal mining potential of the area. He worked for a while as a manager at the

Hendreforgan Colliery, leaving in 1818 before moving on to work at another of his father's coal mines, Lefel yr Office, in Gwter Fawr.

The son's first known purchase of a property was in 1830 when he bought the Cynghordy Farm, Garnant, for £3,900. By 1836 he had seriously started amassing properties: Glynbeudy, Ynys Dawela Farm, Bryn Uchaf and Bryn Isaf farms, Cwmaman Farm and other lands around Gwter Fawr and Gwaun-Cae-Gurwen, as well as houses and cottages and a blacksmith shop. How John Jones was able to afford to buy so much property is speculation. He may have inherited some family wealth.

He also leased the surface and mineral rights of Neyadd Wen, a farm between Brynamman and Garnant. (Surface rights refer to the surface of the land's soil, whereas mineral rights refer to any mineral deposits that have to be drilled for or mined.) He was keen to buy and lease as much land as possible, obviously knowing the potential mineral wealth of the area. In 1828 John Jones Senior had taken out a lease on 120 acres of land in Gwaun-Cae-Gurwen from a Richard H. Lee in order to mine the large coal vein located there. This enterprise was a success and the business was then transferred to his son John.

John Jones probably worked with his father on the construction of the road over the Black Mountain. According to the book, *In the Mist of Time*, written by family descendants, the father financed the road while the son was considered as more directly involved with the road's design and construction. John would have been in his early twenties at the time.

As noted, John inherited Blaencwmteg Farm and Gwter

Fawr Colliery and several annuities from his father. The son also bought Bryn Isaf farm near the River Amman in Gwter Fawr, as its land near the river was a good location to build Brynaman House. The farm had previously belonged to a relative, Owain Jones.

This would appear to be a time of success and profit for the son. Did he use the money left to him by his father to build Brynaman House during 1838/9? He married in 1839, by which time he was nearing his mid forties. According to the 1841 census, he was living in Brynaman House with his wife Elizabeth and a 25 year old named Henry Jones, possibly a relative, plus two servants, and he was described as a coal merchant. His wife came from a family proud of their name and status, the Pendrills / Penderels of Neath. Her parents' gravestone is inscribed: 'The above are all direct descendants of John Penderel of Boscobel.' This John Penderel, known as 'Old John of Boscobel', was a member of a Royalist family who fought alongside King Charles I against Oliver Cromwell and aided him in his escape to France. Charles rewarded the Penderel brothers by giving them and their descendants a pension in perpetuity.

John's prosperity was not to last. In fact, a few years later his fortunes changed dramatically. When his father's business had been branching out from farming to the mineral industry during the Industrial Revolution, a great deal of money was to be made. But John Jones, the son, had to deal with different market conditions in his heyday. Coal mines opening, but then closing and changing ownership was a common occurrence. More risks had to be faced now.

John overstretched his finances; his ambitious and

entrepreneurial ventures needed more capital than he had. This led to him taking out several high rate mortgages, and he even used his mother and younger brother Jonah's assets as security. His difficulties seem to have started at the time he built Brynaman House. He bought several properties, took out leases on others, adding to his costs. He also secured a lease in 1842 on a section of wharf in Llanelli in order to store coal.

His downfall, to a greater extent, was due to his dealings with a Joseph Martin from Swansea. In 1838 he appears to have gone into partnership with him to build an ironworks in Brynaman. But the plan was then put on hold, and by 1840 they were in dispute. Joseph Martin took the matter to court and filed a petition against John Jones. Martin was successful and Jones was ordered to sell several of his properties, agreeing to pay £2,500, plus annual interest, between 1844 and 1846, 'security being all the lands known as Gwter Fawr'.[8] Documents at West Glamorgan Archives in Swansea, the National Library of Wales in Aberystwyth and the National Archives in London show the extent of the mortgages he took out, often at very high punitive interest. One was for £6,850 with Edinburgh Life Insurance.[9]

He also seems to have been a victim of what became known as 'Railway Mania'. This was the downfall of many small and large investors in Britain in the early 1840s. The first railway in Brynaman was the result of Jones's endeavours. According to *Hanes Brynaman 1819–1896*, the railway from Garnant to Brynaman was built by John Jones, the son. This was a branch line of the Llanelly Railway & Dock Company. Subsequently, when the railway bubble burst a few years later, a significant number of investors lost money on shares they bought. This could also have been true for John Jones. Railways were heavily promoted as foolproof financial ventures. Newspapers of the time made it easy for companies to promote themselves to the general public, enticing them to invest, and thousands of investors on modest incomes bought the deposit to a large number of shares. Shares could be purchased for a ten per cent deposit, with the railway company able to call in the remainder of the money promised as investment at any time. Many lost everything when the railway companies called in the remainder of the sums promised.[10]

One penalty John faced for defaulting was his arrangement with the Llanelly Railway & Dock Company. In 1840 an agreement was signed by John and the company with regard to constructing the branch line, including a bridge, at a cost of £3,500 a mile and at his own expense. A clause noted that the construction needed to be completed by 1 February 1841. If there were any delays beyond this date, financial penalties would be incurred on a daily basis. The branch line to carry freight didn't open until June 1842, 16 months later than planned. This, along with defaults in mortgage payments, resulted in John ending up in Carmarthen jail as a bankrupt, as recorded in the 1859 *London Gazette* entry: 'John Jones, late of Brynbrain, out of business – in the gaol of Carmarthen.'[11] Prior to this, he'd lost Brynaman House. One rumour is that he lost it in a bet, but it is probably more likely that he used it as security on a personal loan from another businessman. In all documents available regarding his mortgages and debts, Brynaman House is never listed, which might confirm a personal arrangement was made. He probably sold it to the Amman ironworks as, for many years, managers of the works are recorded as living there in the censuses and family announcement pages of local newspapers.

Therefore, between the cost of building the house, poor investments, speculating activity that went wrong, and overstretching his budget, all these caused a drop in fortune for John Jones. Indeed, this resulted in him having to sell up and move back to live with his mother on the family farm in Brynbrain.

In the 1850s his situation deteriorated badly, both in business and personal life. The 1851 census has him living with his mother at Brynbrain, but his wife is not there. It may be, perhaps, that Elizabeth had left him. Elizabeth is known to have died in 1853. She was not buried in the Pendrill family grave. John's loss of fortune and Elizabeth leaving her husband may have caused a scandal at the time, so perhaps, one can speculate, her family attempted to cover up the details and she moved to live outside the area.

John and Elizabeth had married late in life, while Brynaman House was being built. John was 44, Elizabeth four years older than him having been born 1791. There were no children from the marriage. The 1851 census states that John had an annuity and no other work. Also living at Brynbrain farm then was his bachelor brother and two of his nephews, brother Owen's sons, aged 19 and 22.

In 1863 John was named as executor of his mother Jane's will and was also the sole beneficiary. At first it looked as though she might have lost the farm in her efforts to help her son in his business ventures as, as already noted, she was named as security along with her other son Jonah in mortgage documents dated 1845. However, as also noted,

Brynbrain was never owned by her or her husband John Jones Senior, and this is why it was not listed in his will or as security in her son's business papers. The farm was bequeathed to John Jones Senior's sister Mary who never married, and who had probably cared for their parents and was given the farm as her due. On the 1838 Tithe Map, Mary Jones is listed as the owner and occupier, but she is not recorded on the 1841 census. Jane, who is now a widow, is down as the head of the household in 1841. Mary bequeathed Brynbrain to her nephew, Evan, John Jones Junior's older brother – a common practice at the time when family inheritance was left to the eldest son. Evan lived at Hendreforgan Farm with his family and therefore allowed his mother Jane to live at Brynbrain – perhaps there was a covenant that Jane could live there for her lifetime, as her husband had significantly added to the property.

On Evan's death in 1870, Brynbrain was bequeathed to his two spinster daughters who lived at a hotel in Ferryside. So it was Jonah, their uncle and Jane's youngest son, who moved back to the farm. Jonah died in 1880 and there is an advert for the sale of the farm in 1884, stating a tenant lived there. That would appear to be the end of the line for the Jones family's connection with Brynbrain. An advert in the *Cambrian Daily Leader* for 18 July 1884 offers for sale by auction a 'farmhouse, coach house, stable, other buildings and mineral included'.

John Jones Junior's story in his declining years has him, according to the 1861 census, out of prison. He is recorded as living on the farm in Brynbrain with two female servants and a lodger – John's nephews and Jonah had moved on to live elsewhere. By the 1871 census, John Jones is listed as living with one of his sisters. He is 75 and under 'occupation' is written, 'late colliery proprietor'. John also had a carpentry workshop attached to or near Nantmelyn House off Station Road where his sister Angharad lived. This may have been how he spent his time in later years.

He died on 15 June 1871 at the home of his sister in Brynaman. The *Cambrian Daily Leader*, 19 April 1919, says he died a pauper, but he isn't buried in an unmarked pauper's grave but alongside his older brother Evan in Glanaman Parish Church at Garnant. Evan had lived at Garnant House in the Amman Valley since 1860, dying just a year before John. He had regularly attended the church: 'Mr Jones had a carriage drawn by a horse to convey him and others to Cwmaman Church every Sunday which was used long after the railway came as trains didn't run on Sundays.'[12] Interestingly, he did not belong to one of the Nonconformist chapels built in Brynaman, neither did he choose to travel to the chapel his family had close connections with in Cwmllynfell, which was about the same distance to travel as to the church in Garnant.

According to an article written about John Jones Junior in the *Cambrian Daily Leader*, dated 19 April 1919, he died: 'his means proving sorrowfully unequal to the great feats he ventured.' The article goes on to say that: 'Surviving local elders who lived in the time of the enterprising Jones speak of his name with reverence, and declare that a memorial of some kind ought to have been erected.' Enoch Rees repeats these sentiments in *Hanes Brynaman 1819–1896*. He writes that the community should acknowledge, honour and be proud of those men who had great energy, big hearts and ideas and who engaged in grand adventures despite doubts

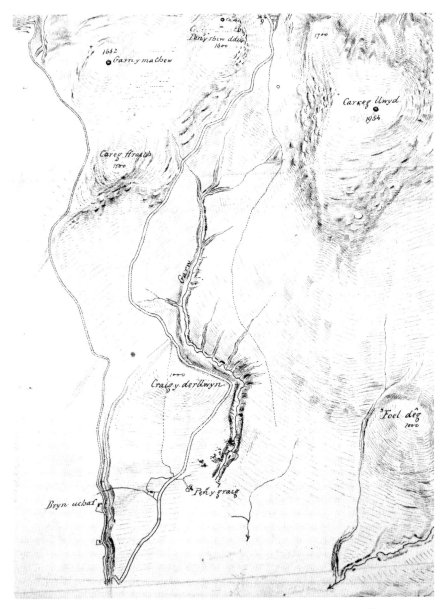

Photograph of a section of an original sketch made of the Black Mountain in 1826. This was used for the first ever Ordnance Survey maps (1830/1). As far as I can discover, this is the first time the Black Mountain road was included on any map. It shows the road going from where Gibea Chapel stands today, past Tro'r Derlwyn. It also shows the older turnpike road.

© British Library Board (shelf mark: Maps 176 Ordnance Survey sketches and revision for 1" 42 & 41, 1826).

Cassini OS Old Series 1830–31 map of the area

© Cassini Publishing Ltd.

Workers at Tro'r Derlwyn in 1914
Courtesy of Treftadaeth Brynaman Heritage

The remnants of the limekilns at the summit of the Black Mountain

The former limestone quarries at the summit

The remnants of the old turnpike road

Commemorative stone to remember an accident on the road in 1884. The road going down towards the Gwynfe side is in the background.

Tro'r Gwcw (cuckoo corner)

Tro'r Derlwyn (oak-grove corner)

Milestone at Tro'r Derlwyn

Milestone opposite Siloam Chapel

Old miners' cottages, Bryn Road

The smithy on Mountain Road which has a blue tin roof, similar to what was described in George Borrow's *Wild Wales*

Road sign on Mountain Road leading into Brynaman

The old chapel in Cwmllynfell

Courtesy of the members of Cwmllynfell Chapel

Bethania Chapel, on the lower slopes of the Black Mountain in Rhosaman

Ebenezer Chapel, Amman Road, Brynaman

Gibea Chapel, on the corner where the Black Mountain road joins Station Road

Hermon Chapel, on Brynaman Road, with Gwaun-Cae-Gurwen Commom behind

Moriah Chapel, Cwmgarw Road, Brynaman

Siloam Chapel, Amman Road, in Lower Brynaman, with the Black Mountain behind and a milestone on the road opposite

Gwynfe's medieval church

Christ Church, Garnant, where
John Jones the son is buried

St Catherine's Church,
Mountain Road, Brynaman

John Jones the elder's gravestone

The inscription on his gravestone

The grave of John Jones the son

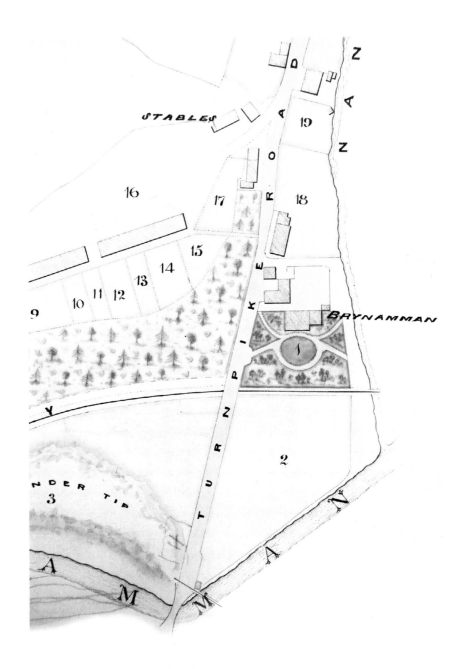

The plan of Brynaman House and garden
© West Glamorgan Archive Service (DD SB 13/E/1)

Brynaman House today

Original fireplace

Internal photographs of
Brynaman House courtesy of
W. Husemann

The stairs and stairwell of
Brynaman House

An arch, alcove and window in Brynaman House

and concerns. These men should have received more respect than they did. According to Enoch Rees, 'the late John Jones Brynbrain, who was in fact the Father of the area, opened up the heart of the area and gave life to Brynaman'.

It's surprising that no monument exists to commemorate both John Joneses. Perhaps, without their efforts to bring the road and railway to the area, the Industrial Revolution would have been delayed significantly there. Would later industrialists who came to the area have risked and invested so much without such local enterprise? Would there have been such a great road over the Black Mountain?

***

The following poem won a prize at Cwmllynfell Eisteddfod in 1859. It is not known which John Jones it is in praise of. The Welsh poem can be found in the book *Canu'r Pwll a'r Pulpud*.[13] The translation tries to convey the meaning.

Penillion o glod i John Jones Brynbrain

Lles a dedwyddwch ei gyd ddynion
Gaiff y lle blaenaf yn ei galon.
Ymdrechodd, do, heb dâl nac elw
I gael ffordd gywrain o Gwm-garw.

Fe roes gynghorion doethion, dethol,
A phob mesurau yn amserol.
Ei gur a'i arian nid arbedoddd
Er gwella'r lleol tra y gallodd.

Fe fyn trafaelwyr, cludwyr clodus
Y wlad, roi iddo'r parch dyledus,
O galon gywir, ddifyr ddefod,
Mewn cân ddifai wrth fynd neu ddyfod.

Verses of praise for John Jones Brynbrain

The benefit and happiness of his fellow man
Are held foremost in his heart.
He attempted, without pay or profit
To build a good road from Cwmgarw.

He gave wise advice when asked for
Always appropriate and timely.
His care and money he didn't hesitate to give
In order to improve the area if he could.

Travellers, carters, people
Everywhere, respected him,
And sang from the hearts his praise
As they came and went on their way.

An interesting footnote to the Jones family's history regards the family Bible that had a record of early names and dates. This Bible was taken or sent to America but was destroyed in the 1906 San Francisco earthquake. William Arthur Jones, a grandson of John Jones Senior, had the Bible in America. He worked in the US Mint and was responsible for guarding gold shipments. His cousin Mary had looked after the family Bible before William had ownership of it. Mary was the daughter of Angharad Watkins, John Jones Junior's sister.

Brynaman House

The house that John the son built in around 1838/9 gave its name to the village when the second railway came to Gwter Fawr in 1864. Brynaman House (first known as just Brynaman) still stands and can be found at the bottom of Station Road. It is now a beautifully restored B&B with its original features remaining. No expense was spared by John Jones when building the house; it has large Georgian windows, decorative alcoves, ceiling roses, cornices, fine fireplaces and a staircase with a double height window in the rear of the house. It is easy to imagine how local miners, in their small two-up two-down cottages, must have thought it a palace, as Enoch Rees suggested in his book. This was the first building in the area to have a slate roof and was also known at the time as *tŷ mawr* (big house) and had beautiful grounds surrounding it.

At the West Glamorgan Archives are plans of the Amman ironworks and farms in the Gwter Fawr area. Dated 1857, they illustrate how Brynaman House had a lawned garden with paths and trees.[14]

The house was built on land, just above the River Amman, which was part of Bryn Bach farm. A second similar palace-like house was not built until 1862, when a Mr Strick built Amman House.[15]

When John Jones's business fortunes declined, it would appear that he either rented the house out, used it to pay a debt, or perhaps sold it to the Amman ironworks. (Of course, there's also the story of him losing it in a bet.) An 1854 newspaper announces the birth of a daughter to the manager of the Amman ironworks, a Mr Henry Richards who lived at Brynaman House. By the 1880s, Mr Strick, another manager, lives at the house. A Mr Hay, also a manager, lived there between 1886 and 1896, followed by Mr Hargreaves who lived there into the 1900s, which assumes that Amman ironworks now owned the property.

The land at the bottom of Brynaman House's garden was later used for the development of the second railway. This could have been because of John Jones's declining fortunes, being that he sold the land to cover his debts. After all the work and expense of building the house, John Jones didn't get to live in it for very long. Brynaman House was a constant reminder of the wealth he had lost.

However, the name he gave his house became the new name for the village, 'thankfully' according to Enoch Rees in his short poem that ends with the following lines:

Wel dyma y flwyddyn, a diolch am hyn
Y claddwyd y Gwter – y codwyd y Bryn![16]

This is the year, thank you for this
The Gwter was buried – but the Bryn raised!

CHAPTER 4

Industrialisation
of Brynaman

As NOTED, JOHN Jones played an important part in constructing the road over the mountain from the small hamlet then known as Gwter Fawr. He also built the road linking the Cwmllynfell area to the Black Mountain road. This chapter will look at how the scattered farms and cottages of the area became the Brynaman village that we know today.

Coal mining in the area goes back to at least the start of the 17th century. As already mentioned, when a baron court was held at Noyadd Wen in 1610, it adjudicated that the coal beneath the ground of the homesteads of tenants of the Manor of Kaegurwen was owned by the tenants, and not by the landlord. The tenant could dig, excavate and sell the coal without the permission of the owner of the land.[1] Before 1700 local farmers excavated coal by surface scouring the various outcrops. The first known deep mine was opened in Glanaman in 1757, although its output was limited and for domestic use only. One of the first collieries in Cwmllynfell was opened in 1798.

The early coal mine owners came from diverse

backgrounds. One coal master, Thomas Walters, was a grocer from Swansea. Richard Aubrey, the owner of Cwmllynfell Colliery by 1830, was a flour wholesaler from Merthyr. Some of the owners of these small coal mines were teachers, solicitors, and even clergy.[2] Coal masters were usually industrialists who had initially become owners of mines in order to ensure control over the supply of coal for their copper and ironworks. John Jones Senior, on the other hand, seemed to have another reason for opening collieries – to supply the already existing but growing lime industry.

As noted, before the railway arrived, Brynaman was known as Gwter Fawr because of a strip-mining method which used a torrent of water to reveal the location of coal seams. In his book *Hanes Brynaman 1819–1896*, Enoch Rees states that the 'Gwter' (channel or gutter) ran from Gorsgoch Uchaf on the edge of Caegurwen Common, past the Old Farmers' Arms (Brynaman Hotel) to the river. In around 1800 there was no village as such, merely a couple of dozen or so farms situated on either side of the River Amman. The first coal mine in Gwter Fawr was opened around 1810 by John Jones Senior when he took out a 30-year lease to open a level. He was the first to dig for coal underground in Gwter Fawr. He opened Lefel yr Office Colliery in 1819. Previously, in 1802, John Jones had opened Blaengurwen Colliery in Rhosaman, and had taken over Hendreforgan Colliery in 1812.

In this area, besides for domestic use, the main market for coal was fuel for the limekilns on the mountain. Each family that worked the seam owned up to six or seven horses to carry the coal to the kilns in summer and then to the homes of Gwynfe village in winter. When the first pits opened, two or three men were employed. Those who worked the coal seam didn't think that anyone from further afield would want to come to develop the area as there was too much of an incline to reach the coal, and no canal to take the coal towards the sea ports.[3] The road, however, changed all that and opened the area up for development.

A rapid expansion of coal extraction followed in the second half of the 19th century. South Wales produced 90 per cent of UK anthracite coal production, and within south Wales almost half of it was mined in south-east Carmarthenshire.[4] In 1837, in a Gwaun-Cae-Gurwen colliery, which came to be known as Old Pit, Richard Hopkin succeeded in reaching the Big Vein of coal which was at sea level.

A Mr Llywelyn was also a major player in the further development of the area. He bought the Gwter Fawr colliery from John Jones and formed the Amman Iron Company in 1847. He went on to build two blast furnaces, as well as houses for workers, adding a forge in 1851 and a third furnace in 1868, which was called the Big Furnace.

When Mr Llywelyn built the two blast furnaces, he attracted 'men from Gwynfe across the mountain' to seek work, according to Enoch Rees. Websites about Llangadog community history note that most of the inhabitants and miners of Brynaman came from Gwynfe originally.[5] But as the Industrial Revolution took hold and more mines and other works opened, men from further afield started coming to the area in search of work, and made it their home. As a result of higher wages being paid to coal workers, men from the iron industry were attracted and started moving into the coal mining villages. Brynaman saw an influx of workers from further afield than just the Carmarthenshire countryside.[6] Later, miners from Merthyr, Aberdare and mid Glamorgan came to the area, with a few Englishmen coming from Somerset and Devon also.

In 1847 some Yorkshiremen called Cleeves, Hardgreaves, Sails, Bartholomew and Sallers, bought a Gwaun-Cae-Gurwen colliery. Frederick Cleeves, along with his son Charles, was especially responsible for expanding the coal trade. The Amman Valley had an impressive reputation worldwide for its Welsh coal, leading to the development of continental trade by the owners of a Gwaun-Cae-Gurwen colliery. Anthracite was in demand to fuel the growing iron industry and coal output trebled in the last decade of the 19th century. And another industrialist, John Hay, opened a lime quarry on the Black Mountain near Blaen Llynfell above Cwmllynfell in 1873.

The Industrial Revolution in the area took not only the form of coal mining but also tin and ironworks, transforming this agricultural area of scattered small farms into a more built-up area that is now Upper and Lower Brynaman.

The successful use of anthracite coal in the manufacture of pig-iron dates from 1838. About this time, iron was smelted by means of hot-blast, and anthracite coal was used for this purpose. In 1839 there were 26 furnaces in operation on the anthracite coalfield. The geographical distribution of the tinplate works in south-east Carmarthenshire in 1880 shows three clusters, one of which was the Amman Valley, including Pantyffynnon, Ammanford, Glanaman and Brynaman. Tinplate was an important part of the economy in the area; at one point there were five tinplate factories in Ammanford and the Amman Valley, with one at Brynaman.

Mines opened, closed and changed ownership often throughout this period. By 1914 there were about 100 privately owned coal mines in the Amman Valley, and the peak in production was around 1920.[7] Enoch Rees, Secretary of the South Wales Coal Federation, was involved in presenting reports about coal mines to various commissions in London. One fascinating fact is that he was 'allowed' to present his report in Welsh![8] And this, possibly, was the first time Welsh had been heard in a formal speech at Westminster Hall.

The coming of the railway

Although industry developed in the area in the early part of the 19th century, with coal mines opened to meet the very local demand of the quarries on the Black Mountain, it was the coming of the railways that encouraged a major expansion of the area. As noted, in 1842 a railway line for freight only was built towards Brynaman to serve the needs of collieries owned by those such as John Jones Brynbrain and the Amman ironworks. The first railway was the Llanelli Railway & Dock Company, later known as Great Western Railway (GWR). This railway had reached Pantyffynon near Ammanford by 1835, reaching, as noted, Brynaman in 1842.

The railway from Garnant to Brynaman had been completed by John Jones Junior as a branch or extension of the Llanelly Railway & Dock Company. Before the railway came to transport coal, horses and carts were used.

At first, the trains were only used for the carriage of

coal and minerals, but passengers were later allowed and
an open passenger carriage was attached to each train,
intended primarily for workmen and their families. Initially
passengers were carried at their own risk, as there was an
absence of stations and a regular timetable. One of the first
records of a passenger journey along the Pantyffynnon to
Brynaman line was written as a diary entry by 16-year-old
Eton schoolboy, Melville Lawford. He visited the Amman
Valley in 1843 and his piece illustrates the danger and dirt
those brave passengers, on a freight service only, had to
endure:

> I went to Cwm Ammon to see a coal mine. We went part of the
> way by train and sat in a rough carriage without buffers next
> to the engine, before it, so that we were continually covered
> with steam & went bump, bump every minute against the
> engine.[9]

This was just the beginning of passengers travelling
alongside the industrial business of the railway. In the
National Archives at Kew there are original letters, dated
1863/4, which passed between the Llanelly Railway & Dock
Company and the Board of Trade at the time, requesting and
being granted permission to carry passengers on the line.
In these documents the railway line is spelt 'Bryn Amman
Branch'. They also mention strengthening a bridge to meet
the demand of increased traffic, even though the railway
itself didn't cross a road. The papers say that no work can
be carried out without the 'consent of the Swansea Vale
Railway Company' regarding the width required. By 1865
the sidings are referred to as Gwter Fawr but the station is
known as Brynaman.[10]

Brynaman was the meeting point for two different railway companies, the Great Western Railway (previously the Llanelly Railway & Dock Company) and the Swansea Vale, known as the Midland Railway from 1874. This line went through Cwmllynfell up to Brynaman. Each company had its own train station which was separated by a road – the two railway lines were never connected. The Midland was built on a dead-end spur. Long-suffering through passengers always had to walk between the two stations according to James Page in *Forgotten Railways: South Wales*. The Midland was much inferior to the GWR because it had not encouraged local passenger traffic and its station remained small, with no shelter for people even. Its line ran up the narrow, twisting, wooded valley of the River Twrch before climbing up to Cwmllynfell. It did not develop its full potential and, as a result, the line from Swansea, with its branch to Brynaman, never developed beyond a local valley railway.[11] When the Swansea Vale Railway station was opened in 1864 and named Brynaman, the name Gwter Fawr itself was changed for ever to Brynaman. The name Brynaman was on the railway station in letters 'big enough to frighten every other name away for ever' according to Enoch Rees![12] Brynaman Post Office opened in 1866; the village was now known officially as Brynaman.

The railways lasted for a hundred years but, as mining in the area went into a gradual decline after the Second World War (with most closing in the 1950s), British Railways abruptly closed the Swansea Valley line on 25 September 1950 and the Pantyffynnon to Brynaman line of the GWR was closed in 1958.

75

Population growth

Brynaman is a perfect example of the impact of industrialisation on an area. The entrepreneurial skills and foresight of a few men, especially the two John Joneses, made this possible. Others were attracted to the area: labourers, miners, mine managers and owners from as far afield as Yorkshire. Even the railways arrived, to what was at the time a remote area, thinly populated with no major road network or navigable river.

Before the middle of the 19th century the majority of people in Wales lived in the countryside, either working on farms or making craft products. By 1851, 35 per cent of the male labour force was employed in agriculture, with only ten per cent employed in the coal industry but, by 1914, the reverse was true.[13]

The 1841 census reflects the increase in the population of Carmarthenshire. In 1801 the population was 71,500 but, by 1841, the figure had risen to 171,000. In barely half a century the population of Carmarthenshire had more than doubled. Most of the population still worked on farms or employment linked to agriculture. However, the higher wages being offered by the collieries and other similar heavy industries drew them away from the countryside. The number of men working in agriculture fell by 38 per cent between 1851 and 1891. According to author Brinley Thomas, 388,000 people migrated from the rural areas of Wales to other parts of the UK between 1851 and 1911, with 320,000 of them going to the south Wales coalfield.[14] The 1851 census shows that the urban population of Britain was larger than that of the rural one.

In 1858 the population of Brynaman was between 800

and 900 but had more than doubled to 2,000 a quarter of a century later.[15] However, one needs to take into consideration the fact that Brynaman lies within two counties, Glamorgan and Carmarthenshire. For example, *Kelly's Trade Directory* records that the 1891 census gave the population as only 1,617. However, this was the population for 'Quarter Bach', which only covers Upper Brynaman. Prior to 1881 'Quarter Bach' was in the parish of Llangadog in Carmarthenshire. Lower Brynaman, on the other hand, was in the county of Glamorgan.

Health

However, the increase in population didn't result in a corresponding increase in social amenities. With relation to health matters, an early 'doctor' in the area was John Jones Senior's son-in-law, the Reverend Rhys Pryse (sometimes spelt Price) who was also the minister at Cwmllynfell Chapel from 1835 to 1869. He was well known for planning his sermons while riding his horse. During his ministry he established prayer meetings and Sunday schools in private houses. He was also known as a bard, carpenter and clog maker and was also a weaver by trade.

A self-taught man of many talents, with E. Griffiths of Swansea he wrote a book about herbal medicine, *Y Llysieu-lyfr Teuluaidd* [Family Herbal Book] in 1849. He was considered an authority on health and his book was used in most homes in the area, a popular source of advice as it was written in Welsh. In the 'Introduction' he writes how he had tried to keep the price of the book low so that it was affordable to most, even the 'dosbarth iselaf' (the lower class). However, a first-edition copy, held at the British

Museum, has gold leaf trim and 29 colour plates of different plants. So the price must have been out of the reach of most families. Nevertheless, it proved to be popular and by the third print, in 1890, the book had a simpler blue cover with the colour pages condensed to just 13 pages.[16]

Despite not receiving any formal education, he had access to reference books and his own book refers to several medical works. His main advice throughout the book is to drink infusions of different kinds of herbs and to eat apples, honey, less meat, and to walk more in the open air – in fact, advice similar to today's way of thinking!

The book reflects the moral attitudes of the time. A man suffering from consumption could be as a result of the fact that he had married too young. 'Green Sickness' afflicted girls who lacked active labour in the open air; it was the result of sitting too long indoors, and wearing clothes that were too tight and damp. The advice was, 'marriage is sometimes the cure against this illness'.[17]

Pryse makes several references to the health of the growing population in the coal mining area. One cause of asthma is due to working in bad air, especially underground. He also comments that Typhus is caused by 'impure air, lack of hygiene and the refuse of so many people coexisting in close proximity'.[18]

The rapid expansion of mining areas created major problems for public health. Overcrowding was a common occurrence when new workers moved into the area, and low-quality housing was quickly erected to accommodate them. Inadequate sanitary conditions made 'towns breeding grounds for disease' in the area.[19] School log books record many epidemics, such as smallpox, diphtheria, measles and scarletina.[20] Brynaman did not escape the illnesses which came with poor living and working conditions, despite its close proximity to open countryside. There was apparently a severe cholera outbreak in 1849 resulting in 20 deaths. The summer of that year also saw a cholera outbreak in other areas, with Carmarthen recording 102 deaths.[21] There was a severe cholera outbreak in other mining areas in 1848/9 too, with over 3,000 people dying of the disease in Glamorgan, with Merthyr Tydfil being the worst hit town.

A Public Health Act, issued in 1848, brought about some improvement in sanitary conditions but the effectiveness depended upon local interest. Between 1848 and 1872 health boards were set up, and they did invest a lot of money in sewerage and water supply. In 1885/6 a waterworks was built to serve the Brynaman area, taking water from several local sources and providing 112 houses with their own private taps, with 28 public taps for general access.[22] A commemorative cast-iron water pump can still be seen on the pavement near Hermon Chapel to mark the location of one of those early clean water taps. Dr Hywel Jones was a local doctor who did a great deal to improve conditions for the community between 1872 and 1904. He was fundamental in getting clean water for the Brynaman, Gwaun-Cae-Gurwen and the Cwmaman areas.[23] Mains sewerage for Upper Brynaman only arrived in the 1920s.[24]

As for another improvement to the living conditions, electricity arrived in the first few years of the 20th century. Gibea Chapel was the first building to have it installed and the electric lights were first turned on for its Sunday service on 2 October 1904. Brynaman Electricity Company had been in existence for a few years already at the time but only supplied street lighting. It took another four years for electricity to reach Gwaun-Cae-Gurwen.[25]

Despite the growing population, the ill health they suffered and frequent injuries, few surgeons are listed in *Kelly's* directories: a David Thomas on Cwmgarw Road in 1889 and an Albert Lewis in 1891. There was a chemist by 1891, along with a 'grocer and medicine vendor'. There are several adverts in newspapers for this chemist dating back to 1887.

Working conditions

Employees had to work extremely long hours. There was child labour down the coal mines, a reliance on company shops for food, and hardships during strike actions. There was industrial unrest during the six-month miners' strike of 1874 in Brynaman and, on 1 March 1880, workers came out on strike for 12 months and five days. As the same company owned the three furnaces and forge in Brynaman, they too had to close down because work had stopped at the colliery.

The Tregib Arms, Cwmgarw Road, in Upper Brynaman, held the first ever local union branch meeting to look after the needs of Welsh anthracite miners in 1891. The original notice about this still hangs on a wall in the pub's foyer.

Enoch Rees, in his capacity as Secretary for the South Wales Coal Federation, put forward a motion to the Labour Congress of 1891, held in London, that a person should pass some sort of examination before being allowed to work underground, so dangerous was the work. However, he added, 'except those that started working very young, because an inexperienced worker can make a mistake in his ignorance which could endanger the lives of hundreds of his co-workers'. Enoch Rees had been 'born and raised at the coalface'.[26]

Boys, as well as men, worked between nine and eleven hours a day. Collieries, as a rule, commenced work at six o'clock in the morning, and worked until five. It was the custom in the region to work ten or even 12 hours a day. An example of this is the largest colliery in the Gwaun-Cae-Gurwen area which was well known for its long hours. On top of a lengthy working day, Enoch Rees points out that men often had to walk great distances to their work. He cites some men walking an hour and a half to work each day, and then another hour and a half to get back home.

As for women and children working in coal mines, it would appear that the Amman Valley and Carmarthenshire area may not have been the worst area for this. There were poor conditions in other places such as Pembrokeshire and the eastern coalfield in Monmouthshire where very young children were expected to work. Women didn't work underground in the Gwaun-Cae-Gurwen area but they did work on the surface at nearby Cwmgors.[27] Very young children opened ventilation doors, thus helping their fathers. In 1842, a Parliamentary Act was passed excluding women and children under ten from underground work at collieries, although it was generally slow in being implemented and boys continued working in Gwaun-Cae-Gurwen until 1856. However, the practice had largely died out by 1850 when overmen were responsible for seeing that there was compliance with the law. In 1872 the Mines' Regulations Act compelled children who worked in coal mines to go to school for ten hours a week.[28]

However, this impacted on a family's income. Statistical accounts of miners' wages are difficult to gauge, due to the ups and downs of the market price of coal, the 'drab and boom' times as they were called. During the 'drab' period in trade in 1859, for example, colliers' estimated wage was only three shillings a day in Carmarthenshire and four shillings in Glamorganshire. In the 'boom' period that followed, Rhondda men earned 35 shillings a week. Miners' standard of living fluctuated with market forces.[29]

Housing

At the beginning of the 19th century there were 21 dwellings (farmhouses, cottages and crofts) along the River Amman in what was then known as Gwter Fawr.

The earliest date on a house on a main road in Brynaman is 1813, located on Station Road: 'This house was built by me Owen Jones in 1813.' It appears to have once been the farmhouse of Bryn Isaf Farm, and is next door to Brynaman House. However, there was once also a house in existence in the early 1800s called Cwmgarw (on the Carmarthen side of the River Amman) that was thought, locally, to have been 400 years old at the time. Evidence of this house has long gone. Apparently, three large stones made up one corner and there were oak beams in the loft.[30]

Small houses on the edge of the mountain, on the road between Rhosaman and Cwmllynfell, were once built in the old Welsh tradition of *tŷ unnos*, that is, a house built overnight between sunset and sunrise. These overnight houses were, by their nature, hastily erected, and were usually made of turf and soil or any stones found nearby, and had a rough thatched roof. Smoke had to rise out of the chimney by daybreak to signal that the house was finished. The family was then allowed to live in the house. There are a few of these original *tai unnos* remaining but have now been altered and modernised over the years.

The first miners' cottages to be built were called Tai'r Office (Office Houses) as one of the houses was the pay office for the miners. Initially, 15 miners were employed by John Jones at his mine with some, if not all of them, living in these houses. These houses were later buried under a tip and Enoch Rees notes that the tip was called Pencraig in 1888.[31]

A feature of housing in this part of the south Wales coalfield is the absence of many mansion-type houses overshadowing coal miners' terraced houses, unlike that which happened in the large towns of the iron industry.[32] Of course, owners and managers did live in bigger and better buildings than their workforce. An interesting factor, however, is that coal owners and their managers were often local men who worshipped in the same chapels as their workers. As noted, this was true of John Jones Brynbrain who was a deacon at his local chapel in Cwmllynfell and remained on the family farm all his life. However, his son did build a mansion.

The 19th century saw many attracted to the area as they searched for work. Cottages were built by companies to house their workers. Both Upper and Lower Brynaman are characterized by their long, linear rows of cottages, with some detached and semi-detached houses. A good example of an old miner's cottage is on Bryn Road, and there's also a row of four old cottages halfway up Station Road.

Miners' cottages were usually solidly built, as good

building materials were readily available – fire clay and brick works were often found near collieries. Miners' cottages often had three or four rooms and, if not overcrowded, were comfortable and superior to the dwellings of rural west Wales. For example, early houses in rural Carmarthenshire had mud walls or walls made of local stone. Instances of these very early rural domestic architecture do not appear to have survived in the Brynaman area. As well as the *tŷ unnos*, the type of dwelling that did exist before industrial growth led to many *tŷ to cawn*, a house with a roof made of rushes, being erected.[33] These houses had one floor, with a door, one or two windows about eight inches square, and a chimney made of twisted wicker or straw.

An example of a small stone and thatch cottage from rural Carmarthenshire, built in the 1770s, has been reconstructed at St Fagans National Museum of History near Cardiff. Its original site was at Taliaris, about 15 miles from Brynaman on the other side of the Black Mountain. It probably closely resembles the type of pre-industrial dwelling that could once have been found in the Gwter Fawr area. If you look closely at some outbuildings or old garages in Brynaman, there are traces of what could have been early dwellings – a small chimney indicating their original use as a home.

The experience and conditions of living in more urban areas, as compared to the rural life that many workers had come from, must have been very different. The miners' terraces built to house workers would have been very modern by comparison to rural dwellings. In 1881 grey stone from the Black Mountain was also used for building St Catherine's Church.[34] According to George Borrow, who visited in 1854:

Gutter Vawr consists of one street, extending for some little way along the Swansea road, the foundry, and a number of huts and houses scattered here and there. The population is composed almost entirely of miners, the workers at the foundry, and their families... beyond the grove a range of white houses with blue roofs, occupied, I suppose, by miners and their families.[35]

In 1848 the Amman Iron Company built Tai'r Cwmni (Company Houses), a row of 20 houses above the Great Western station. In 1865 the Llywelyn family built six houses near the ironworks. Some houses were also built around this time near the Tregib Arms in Upper Brynaman and five houses were built on Station Road. In 1872 a Mr Strick had 20 houses, called Tinmen's Row, built for his workers. A further 20 were built two years later on what is now called Chapel Street.[36] The Amman Iron Company, under Mr Strick's direction, built several more houses for the tinplate workers; 20 houses in Cannon Row (now called Cannon Street) were built by the company in 1873 'mainly for miners and their families'.[37] By 1874 the company had built about 82 houses in total in the area. This was the beginning of the housing boom. In 1860 there had been 146 houses, but by 1896 it had more than doubled to 380.[38]

Brynaman did not grow into a large town, probably due to the geography of the valley which was not wide enough for a large urban sprawl. Similar geography explains why Rhondda's large villages grew, not towns: 'chains of villages and no street more than a few steps away from open mountain.'[39] True of the Brynaman area as well, and characterised by the continuous rows of houses all the way from Hermon Chapel to Rhosfa Road, for two and a quarter miles, only in a few parts do other roads link into the main road, for example Barry Road in Lower Brynaman, and New Road in Upper Brynaman. The close proximity of the mountain is very apparent from Rhosfa Road on towards Cwmllynfell.

However, what seems a pleasant location today isn't to say that housing conditions were very good during the area's development into a coal mining village. An interesting article in *The Cardiff Times*, dated 1909, illustrates how finding enough housing to accommodate miners and their families in this boom period was an ongoing problem. Large families crammed into these small houses, and even lodgers were taken in as well. One headline stated 'Brynaman house famine' and described the problem as follows:

> There is a great scarcity of dwellings at Brynaman. On the Black Mountain side of the town a number of families have erected a shelter for themselves by means of corrugated iron sheets, which are always available in districts where the tin-plate industry flourishes, whilst on the Glamorgan side some families are camping out, having pitched their tents on the common land... there are scores of families in apartments, and the same conditions prevail at Ammanford. A policeman remarked that he found no fewer than 30 of the tramping labourer class sleeping out at the brickworks and tinworks in the district... an empty House is hard to find.

Lack of housing seemed to have been a constant problem as early as 1846 when Daniel Williams, in his essay, comments that it was hard to find a place to live as few houses had been built by then. Even after a further 18 dwellings were built in 1849, this was not enough to solve the problem.[40] More houses were subsequently built as a result of the cholera outbreak of 1849. However, today, if you walk from where the Gwter once was at the start of Amman Road, up Station Road to the start of the Black Mountain road and the old tollhouse, there are many missing numbers between some houses. Many original miners' cottages have long gone, along with the old rural cottages that once existed, making room for more recent development.

Waking up on a cold, wet or misty morning, the mountain might have felt oppressive to some miners and villagers, especially faced with the black tips on their doorstep. The name Black Mountain would have seemed appropriate, although the name more likely derived from the blackness of the peatbogs. In contrast, on a clear sunny day the prospect of a walk up to breathe in mountain air might have helped to clear the dust from their lungs. If they were able to reach the summit and look down on the green fields where most had come from, this would have conjured up the feeling of *hiraeth*, a longing for their previous way of life – until they remembered the harsh reality of the poverty that had driven them off the land.

The road across the mountain was the beginning of industrial growth in the area but also contributed to social change as it improved social mobility for more rural communities.

CHAPTER 5

Brynaman's social, religious and cultural development

IT WASN'T JUST the mine and ironworks' entrepreneurs who helped develop Brynaman and its near neighbours' economy. People of commerce, trade and other businesses met the needs of the growing population. The social and cultural development of those living in the area was important too, with the founding of chapels and churches meeting religious needs.

The area's population was almost stagnant between 1550 and 1800. However, with the Industrial Revolution it increased rapidly, with a significant change seen in the social and cultural life of the area. House building had a profound effect on the locality, with farms and the agricultural way of life declining, indeed some farms disappearing altogether.[1] Some miners did hold on to or established smallholdings, maintaining their links to farming, as it could supplement their wages. Rhosaman, with its scattered cottages and pieces of land on the very edge of the open mountain, is an example of this and the evidence can still be seen to this day.

Language

The Welsh language was an integral part of not only the home and chapel but also the workplace at this time. Welsh had not been 'weakened' or taken over by the use of English, despite all the new workers migrating to the area to find work. In fact, it's quite significant how migrant miners from Yorkshire learnt to speak Welsh. George Borrow makes an interesting remark in his book *Wild Wales*. He describes his experience of travelling through Gwter Fawr in the 1850s and encountering a 'respectable man' who showed him around the iron foundry. Borrow asked him if there were any English employed on the premises. 'None,' said he, 'nor Irish either; we are all Welsh.' Borrow goes on to comment, 'Though he was a Welshman, his name was a very common English one.'[2]

Between 1900 and 1914 English workers from Lancashire came in their droves to the area. For example, the Wigan Coal and Iron Company owned mines in Brynaman. With the Welsh language and culture very strong, they rapidly learned the language and were assimilated well into the local community. Welsh was the language of the coalface, and mines had Welsh names too.[3]

Enoch Rees, in his position as Secretary for the South Wales Coal Federation, reported to the Labour Congress in 1891 that 95 per cent of the population of the Brynaman area were Welsh speakers.[4] Coalfield immigrants from outside Wales did encounter barriers: 'peasants from the counties of Cardigan, Carmarthen and Pembroke could get employment more readily. Cornish miners who talked and worked in different ways would not understand instructions when given.' In the west of Wales, apart from a few overmen brought in for their technical knowledge, English workers were 'rarely to be found'.[5]

Religion and Nonconformist Chapels

Nonconformist denominations came into being from the 17th century onwards as a result of differing theological interpretations of scripture and worship from that of the Established Church. The main 17th-century Nonconformist religious sects were Baptists, Presbyterians and Independents (also known as Congregationalists), together with the much smaller Society of Friends, or Quakers. Most of these played a part in the religious history of Wales.

The history of Nonconformity in Wales is one of a steady increase in popularity during the 18th century, with greater growth in the 19th century. Villages and towns had at least one chapel, often several. This religious activity saw a huge increase in membership amongst the Nonconformist denominations, which in turn led to a great wave of chapel building across the country. This was to last throughout the 19th century and into the early 20th century. Brynaman, along with the neighbouring villages, with its total of six chapels, is a good example of this. During this period it has been estimated that, on average, a chapel was being built in Wales every eight days, and it is thought that the combined seating capacities of all these chapels may have exceeded the number of people actually living in Wales. This resulted in one of the most obvious architectural features in Welsh villages and towns, the chapel. The new communities that emerged out of the Industrial Revolution provided even more opportunities for chapel building.[6]

Revivalism was a feature of Nonconformity. There was

a powerful Revival in 1859 and an even more remarkable one in 1904–5, the largest Christian Revival in Wales. The Revival of 1904 began under the leadership of Evan Roberts (1878–1951), a 26-year-old former collier and minister in training. The Revival lasted less than a year, but in that time 100,000 people were converted.[7]

Nonconformity didn't comment on the relationship between religious belief and entrepreneurial activity, but a great many coal mine owners in the south Wales coalfield were Nonconformist.[8]

Chapels were built in the area from the early 1700s. Prior to any chapels being built in the upper part of Brynaman, people travelled to Cwmllynfell, while those living in the lower part of Brynaman went to Hen Bethel which is located above Garnant in the Amman Valley. Hen Bethel was built in 1773 and was the first dedicated place of worship in the Amman Valley. Its cemetery is still used for burials to this day.

Chapels had a considerable influence and raised the moral standards of the mining community. According to a Royal Commission Trade Unions' Report in 1867–8, the Nonconformist minister exercised 'far more influence than his master'[9] on the miner. What marked newcomers to the area out from the typical Welsh miner was their 'low moral standard, the influence exercised on the Welsh collier by his religious belief' according to a *Western Mail* article in 1871.

Brynaman, with its linear development, has all of its chapels along the main roads. Gibea, the first chapel built, in 1842, is on Mountain Road but, because of the increase in population due to expanding industry, a larger chapel was necessary. In 1856 a new Gibea Chapel was built for the Independent denomination. The Methodists built Moriah on Cwmgarw Road in 1871. Baptist chapel Siloam, on Amman Road, was built in 1872. Anglican church St Catherine's, just off the bottom of Mountain Road, was built in 1881. And, with the building of a new tinplate works in Lower Brynaman, there was a demand for a new chapel and Independent chapel, Ebenezer, was opened on Amman Road in 1882 as an extension to Gibea. Bethania Chapel was also an extension of Gibea and was built in 1905 and located on the road to Cwmllynfell. Lastly, Hermon was built for the Independents in Lower Brynaman in 1909 on the common that separates Brynaman from Gwaun-Cae-Gurwen.

As well as services on Sundays, chapels held different themed meetings during the week. There were also annual events to prepare for, involving rehearsals for weeks in advance – the two most significant being the 'Gymanfa Ganu' (hymn singing festival) and Eisteddfod (a Welsh-language festival of music, poetry, drama and art).

Cwmllynfell Independent Chapel

Cwmllynfell Independent Chapel, where John Jones's family worshipped for generations and where John Jones Senior was deacon and chapel secretary, is closely linked to the early history of Welsh Nonconformity.

An original document, held at the West Glamorgan Archives in Swansea and dated September 1754, grants land for a meeting house to be built for use by 'Protestants, Dissenters or Prespiterians'. It was granted for a 'thousand years', paying a rent of a penny a year. This deed was between the landowner, Thomas Pryce, Parish of Cadaxton, Glamorgan, and a group of eight men, presumably the first chapel's deacons.[10] The meeting house was to be located in Cwmllynfell at a place called Bryn and was to have a thatched roof.

A chapel is known to have been built later, in 1786, and perhaps replaced this earlier meeting house. The chapel was then rebuilt in 1814 and further extended in 1861. An image of this chapel hangs in the foyer of the present-day chapel, showing a large two-storey building with a slate roof. This is the chapel John Jones attended and was buried at in 1835. The chapel, together with its graveyard, is a derelict ruin near the river now. It's surprising that the ruin and cemetery exist at all today, having avoided being demolished by the nearby mining development or flooded by the river, as well as having to make way for the railway cutting nearby. Local developers of mines and railways must have respected this old place of worship.

The 1786 chapel played an important role in the area's early religious and cultural history. A full history of the chapel, in Welsh, can be found in Rev. J.D. Owen's book, *Hanes Eglwys Cwmllynfell* (1935), which is available in Carmarthen Library's archives and at the National Library of Wales. For two hundred years, from the mid 17th century, the Independents were the only religious body in the Cwmllynfell and Brynaman areas.

As early as 1648, the population of Cwmllynfell had come under the influence of Huw Edwards, the Puritan pastor at Llanddeusant and Llangadog. The first minister at Cwmllynfell was Llewelyn Bevan, and he served between 1701 and 1724. Preachers from Cwmllynfell visited Gwynfe during the 1730s.[11] At this time many people in the area were moving away from the preaching of the Anglican Church and towards Nonconformist worship, and met in secret on farms on the Gwrhyd Mountain above Cwmllynfell.

Shops and businesses

As more miners took advantage of work in the area, a wide range of shops and services flourished to meet the needs of the growing population. At its peak Brynaman had 150 different traders and businesses, ranging from a small sweet shop in a wooden building to a large drapers' shop called London House at the top of Station Road.[12]

The first shop was established in around 1828/31. Twm o'r Gat sold soap, cheese, butter, tea, sugar, tobacco and candles, obviously that which was considered as essential in those days. During this early period if anything could not be grown or obtained locally, people had to travel all the way to Llandeilo, ten miles away, where flour, salt, starch, wheat and barley could be bought.

John Jones's eldest daughter, Angharad, and her husband Mr Watkins, had a drapers' shop in Gwter Fawr according to the 1861 and 1871 censuses. Enoch Rees's book says that their shop was the first 'proper' shop in the community and the second building in the area to have a slate roof – it having been built in around 1839. It was called simply 'Siop Watkins'. Prior to this a Mr Hopkins had 'some kind of shop' in Glynbeudy, whereas the Watkins' shop sold everything and was 'full of all kinds of goods'. It would appear that the first postal service was operated from these premises, before moving in 1866 to the top of Station Road.

Early tradesmen were often versatile, like David Francis,

a smithy who came to Brynaman from Gwynfe in about 1870 and had a workshop on Mountain Road. He wasn't just a farrier but also pulled teeth, cut hair and even held a Sunday school for 15 children.[13]

The controversial Company Shop, or Truck System, was in place in Brynaman between 1850 and 1865. The truck system meant that workers were paid in a currency substitute, such as vouchers or token coins, known in some dialects as 'scrip' or 'chit'. These tokens were exchangeable for goods at the company store, often at highly-inflated prices. This limited workers' ability to choose how to spend their earnings, as the company vouchers could only be used at a company-owned stores. The system was exploitative because there was no competition to force lower prices and consumers could also be in debt to the shop. These shops were later controlled by the Truck Acts of 1887 and 1896 which prevented employers misusing wage-payment systems to the detriment of their workers.[14] Cooperatives, run by their own members, then became popular, distributing a share of profits according to purchases that came to be known as the 'divi'. The Co-operative movement grew from a small shop in Lancashire in 1844, becoming worldwide eventually, and a Co-operative Society store opened in Brynaman in 1876.

The earliest trade directory[15] to list Brynaman's shops and businesses was *Worrall's Trade Directory* of 1875. It describes Brynaman as a large village and gives the names of some shopkeepers and tradespeople. Later directories, such as *John Wright & Co.'s Swansea & South Wales Trade Directory* of 1889, along with *Kelly's Directory of Monmouthshire and South Wales* for 1891, give more details. Kelly's list for

Brynaman includes 11 grocers, four drapers, two butchers, a stationer, three ironmongers, one hardware store and a house furnisher. There was also a bookseller, a beer retailer and a 'chemist and agent for wine and spirits', as well as a 'coffee tavern' near the railway stations. Five 'shops' are undefined as to what exactly they sold. Often these kinds of shops were opened in the 'front' room of houses. Other traders listed were three bootmakers, a tailor, blacksmith, stonemasons and carpenter. Most of these shops and trades were to be found on Station Road and Cwmgarw Road, with a few at the bottom of Mountain Road and others on Llandeilo Road and the bottom of the Old Turnpike Road. *John Wright & Co.'s Swansea & South Wales Trade Directory* (1889) lists a grocer who was also a 'patent medicine vendor', and a Mrs Goode Evans who was a professor of music. There were two post offices by 1889, one in Lower Brynaman on Park Street, as well as one on Station Road. By 1903 there were two solicitors and an insurance company, a newsagent, two china dealers, three confectioners, a saddler, a leather merchant, a tobacconist and two more coffee taverns had opened. These trade directories show the extent to which Brynaman had grown.

Treftadaeth Brynaman Heritage Group has collected material for the Community Archives Wales Project. They have researched the changing nature of shops and businesses in Brynaman, and have an extensive collection of receipts, photographs, letters and artefacts.[16]

Banks

At one time Brynaman had three banks on Station Road. One of the earliest banks, according to Enoch Rees, was a branch of the Glamorganshire Bank, established in the house of the chemist in 1889. Other banks which had branches in the village at one time or another were the Midland Bank, Barclays Bank and Lloyds Bank on Mountain Road. Trade directories for 1900 and 1903 list one bank, the Capital and Counties Bank Limited.

Prior to the banks opening, there were 'friendly societies' which were often based in pubs. For example, the Bristol & West Friendly Society was to be found at the Tregib Arms in Upper Brynaman, and The Oddfellows Philanthropic Friendly Society in the Farmers' Arms from 1860 onwards. They provided a form of insurance, paid out to workers at times of sickness or when unable to work.[17]

Post Office

By the 1860s the name Gwter Fawr was being used less frequently, with the name Brynaman used much more commonly. As noted, when the Swansea Vale Railway opened its station in the village of Gwter Fawr in 1864, the name of the new railway station was Brynaman, and this was also the name printed on tickets. Then, in 1866, 'Brynaman Post Office' opened, and a gradual transition of the village name changing from Gwter Fawr to Brynaman was under way. There had also previously been a post office at a different location on Station Road. Another post office was later established on Park Street in Lower Brynaman.

In 1866 it took three days for the mail from London to arrive in Carmarthen at a 'prescribed rate of travelling five miles an hour'. For example, on 26 December 1866, the post left London at two in the afternoon and arrived in Carmarthen on 29 December at 9.30 in the morning.[18] With the advent of the railway, of course, it arrived much faster. At the beginning of the 19th century, the closest local post office to receive mail from London was Llangadog or Neath, and it would cost 10*d*. for that journey. If you needed to send mail locally, a distance of less than 15 miles, then it would cost 4*d*.[19]

Schooling

The first schooling available in the area was the circulating schools held by the Reverend Griffith Jones between 1730 and 1761. These religious schools were conducted in Welsh and travelled from village to village, operating only between September and May so that they didn't interfere too much with agricultural work. According to Enoch Rees, the first school in Brynaman, in 1823, was run by local blacksmith Evan Williams. But he also sold beer at the establishment! Then, in 1825, some kind of school was held in an old cottage near Gwter Fawr by a Dafydd Williams; he provided slates and large A, B and C cards. A school was also run from a room in the Farmers' Arms at one point.

Sunday schools existed by around 1841[20] and offered informal Welsh-language education, covering theology and poetry. Many learnt to read at Sunday school and, unlike in other countries, both adults and children attended in Wales as it was held on a Sunday, a non-working day. The education received at Sunday schools helped 'induce enthusiastic warmth of religious feeling in the absence of crime'.[21] This lack of crime was commented upon by Enoch Rees. In the 60 years between 1820 and 1880 when Brynaman was growing apace, apart from strikes, there hadn't been any 'murders or bad events' to record; rather it was a peaceful, quiet, law-abiding place whose inhabitants were 'highly moral and religious'.[22]

Welsh was the language of the Nonconformist chapels. Owning a copy of the Welsh Bible and mastering its contents was expected.

Welsh schools in the mid 19th century were the subject of a Commission set up to visit all parts of Wales in 1846 and present its findings. The report, which became known as the Treachery of the Blue Books (*Brad y Llyfrau Gleision*), stated that schools in Wales were extremely inadequate and that Welsh speakers had to rely on Nonconformist Sunday schools to acquire literacy. The report was critical of the Welsh language and Nonconformity, but it had relied a great deal on the comments of those who belonged to the English Established Church. As a result, there was a strong reaction that could be regarded as an early catalyst for Welsh self-government.[23]

John Jones Junior apparently sponsored a school, although it is not clear which one. In 1856 the new Gibea Chapel was built, and the old chapel was turned into a formal school. Possibly this is the building seen in the overgrowth at the north end of the cemetery; it has a large decorative window. The building measured 30 by 24 feet, making it substantial enough to house 100 to 150 pupils. A purpose-built new school was erected opposite Gibea Chapel, and was partly maintained by contributions from men employed by the Amman ironworks company. From 1 April 1893, this school became known as the Llandilo Fawr Urban District Brynaman Board School. It was enlarged in 1903 but the building burnt down in 1940. A new school was built in Cwmgarw Road in 1946. This is the location of the Black Mountain Centre today.

Kelly's Directory for South Wales and Monmouthshire for 1895 records that the Board School had 295 children, with average attendance being 154 boys and 113 girls. School numbers then increased rapidly and, by 1910, the same volume records 483 pupils. With increasing population, a second school was built in 1896 in Lower Brynaman by the Llangiwg School Board, which had to be enlarged 13 years later in 1909.

Entertainment

Eisteddfod competitions were an important source of entertainment in the area, especially competitions between the chapels of Brynaman. Such events started when men interested in literary matters met in private houses to discuss each other's poetry. These small, informal poetic or literary competitions were held on farms which had suitable large barns to host them, such as those in Rhosfa and Rhosaman. Some of these meetings developed into local eisteddfodau in the villages of the district. One poet, D.L. Moses from Cribyn, Cardiganshire, came to work as a clerk in the Amman ironworks in 1840, later teaching the principles of Welsh bardic strict metres and encouraging men to compete in local eisteddfodau. Eisteddfodau proliferated from 1857 onwards, with large ones held in Brynaman in 1859, 1871, 1881, 1884 and 1887. One which drew comment from the newspapers of the time, and in Enoch Rees book, was held in 1884. A large tent was erected in the school playground, and 3,000 people were able to be seated in it. Here 'so many of the working classes gathered together, they were a credit to the country and a class of people'.[24] Eisteddfodau were even held on Christmas night, as in 1897 at the old public hall, the Alpha.

Choirs and brass bands were particularly popular in Brynaman and the surrounding valleys. Over the years there were various bands: brass, banjo, mouth organ, an orchestra, operatic society, as well as chapel choirs and drama groups.[25]

Public Hall

No account of the history of Brynaman can omit mentioning its public hall which, today, has a large cinema screen showing up-to-the-minute films. Despite cinema multiplexes being built and small cinemas closing, Brynaman's still continues.[26]

The present public hall traces its origins back to the 1920s when it was funded by the 'check-off' system, one whereby weekly contributions were deducted from miners' wages. Initially, this was to build the hall, but subsequently the monies were used to run it. Building work started in 1924, and the official opening ceremony was on 15 May 1926. It could seat around 1,100 people.

There had been a previous public hall and cinema called the Alpha which was located on Station Road. This was made of wood and zinc sheets. Dramatically, it burnt down in 1915 and 900 books were among the contents lost in the fire.[27] It was a substantial building, with five shops at street level.

The new hall built to replace it also had a library and lounge where miners could relax or play cards around the oak tables. There was also a billiard room above the library.

The cinema showed silent films until the 1930s, then 'talkies' became popular; concerts and plays were also held. The hall was the location of the annual finale of the inter-chapel Eisteddfod, with the main hall furnished throughout with tip-up upholstered seats. Bethania Chapel, in Rhosaman, has very comfortable church pews with gold and brown velour covers which were bought from the cinema.[28]

Newspapers

Newspapers were not easily accessible at the beginning of the 19th century. However, a newspaper article from 26 December 1889 in *Tarian y Gweithiwr*, 'The Old Chapel in Cwmllynfell 50 years ago', says that John Jones Brynbrain was the only member to receive a weekly newspaper and he shared the week's news with others as they left chapel on a Sunday. His preferred newspaper was *The Cambrian*, it having been established in 1804. It was the first weekly newspaper to be published in Wales. Around 50 years later, by 1856, very many newspapers and journals were delivered to Brynaman: 18 daily, 198 weekly and 96 monthly papers. And by the end of the century this had increased to 39 daily, 715 weekly and 129 monthly papers.[29]

Pubs

The first pub in the area, the Farmers' Arms, opened in 1823. 'Yr Hen [Old] Farmers', as it became known, was located where the gutter entered the river in Lower Brynaman.

This pub was then replaced by the New Farmers' Arms which was built in 1840 near the bridge which crosses the river, only a few hundred yards away. This new pub was only the third building in the area with a slate roof. Baptist meetings were held in the clubroom, or Long Room, of the New Farmers' Arms at no charge, with minister Mr Edwards travelling there from Pontardawe. Baptisms were carried out in the river at 'Pwll y Cwar' near the bridge. A Baptist chapel wasn't built until 1872.[30]

The travel writer George Borrow describes aspects of Gwter Fawr and his overnight stay at the Farmers' Arms in 1854.[31] This was probably the New Farmers' Arms (nowadays Brynaman Rugby Club). The Old Farmers was rebuilt in 1894 and was renamed to Brynaman Hotel. At the back of the building one can still see a sign, 'Brynaman Hotel', in big black letters.

The Colliers' Arms was the next pub to be built in 1838 in Lower Brynaman. This was then followed by The Crown in 1847, again in Lower Brynaman, with it being rebuilt many times over the years, lastly in 1914. The Tregib Arms was another early pub on the Cwmgarw Road in Upper Brynaman, and that was built around 1860, with the Gwyn Arms being built on the same road in 1868. There was also the Derlwyn Arms on Mountain Road, along with the Black Mountain Inn as well.

The social effect of the railway

The railways not only had a dramatic impact on the economic life of the area but also offered significant social benefits. Residents of Brynaman and the other villages were now less isolated and had smoother access to the rest of the country and further afield. Markets in Llanelli, Carmarthen and Swansea were easy to get to, as well as social activities like the dance hall in Ystalyfera. This also meant that paid work could be obtained away from the area, and social mobility was now a possibility. The demand for labour in other Welsh coalfields resulted in many journeys being 'all too frequently one way'.[32]

***

To sum up how the area grew: in 1847 Gwter Fawr had two shops, four pubs, one place of worship and no school. Forty years later, by the end of the 1880s, Brynaman had approximately 28 shops, seven pubs, four places of worship, and a school. The population was around 2,000, with 380 private houses. More roads were built and named and, by 1896, the following can be identified: Heol y Mynydd Du, Heol Cwmgarw, Heol Llandeilo, Heol y Bryn, Heol y Parc, Heol Glynbeudy, Heol y Cwar and Station Road. However, Brynaman never became a town and had no town hall, civic centre or a town square.

Therefore, Gwter Fawr, an area which wasn't even a hamlet or village in the 1760s at the beginning of the Industrial Revolution, grew into a large elongated village. By 1860 various mines and ironworks, along with the introduction of the railway, brought different trade and commercial businesses, meeting the needs of the vastly growing population. Chapels were built and flourished. At its peak, towards the end of the 19th century and early 20th century, the village of Brynaman had every shop and trade a *town* could provide.

This remarkable growth did bring with it its problems of poor living and working conditions. But it also developed a cultural and religious character that has made Brynaman and its near neighbours what they are today. Rhosaman,

Cefnbrynbrain, Cwmllynfell, Gwaun-Cae-Gurwen, Cwmgors, Garnant – all these villages and others in the Amman Valley have an enterprising story to tell.

6

Conclusion

'Great things are done when men and mountains meet' claimed William Blake.[1] This account of how Brynaman came to be, and the industrialisation that followed building the road over the Black Mountain, is a story of interrelated events that have left a permanent mark on the people and landscape of this small corner of Wales.

Wales was the first industrial nation, having a slate industry in north Wales, the south-eastern coalfield of Merthyr and the Rhondda, and Swansea and Morriston's Copperopolis. Less recognition, however, has been given to the early history of the Amman Valley, especially the contribution of the lime industry and its influence in developing coal mining on a greater scale to supply the kilns.

In J.H. Morris & L.J. Williams's book, *The South Wales Coal Industry 1841–1875*, written in 1958 just as the coal mining industry was starting to decline, there is an interesting quote from a report to a 1945 Technical Advisory Committee:

> The years of which we write... were the days of the pioneer... we must point out the mistakes which were made in these

early years of the coal mining industry, but let us beware of merely being wise after the event, or of withholding the need of praise due to a great race of men, employers, mining engineers, workmen and machinery makers alike. For whatever their faults, they were fit to rank with the greatest of Britain's industrial pioneers... the best of them showed initiative and perseverance in gaining new markets. It would be unfair to say all their endeavours could be seen as self-interest, their characteristics made such men natural leaders and might have regarded some of what they did as a public duty not just private gain.

Not every early entrepreneur became a well-known character of the Industrial Revolution. Some are only remembered in local histories, with many names being lost as bigger businesses or companies took over their works. For many of them, even the details of their work and contribution to the community have been lost in the mists of time. John Jones Senior and Junior were held in high esteem by their peers and community. We will never know exactly what kind of men they were or what drove them. They can be described as early entrepreneurs, without whom the mountain road would not exist as it does today and Brynaman's history might have taken a very different course.

***

Looking down from the Black Mountain over Brynaman, it's hard to imagine the noise described by George Borrow as he approached what was then known as Gwter Fawr by road in the 1850s. All signs of furnaces, mines and railways have gone. Ynys Dawela Nature Park in Brynaman is an example of how nature can reclaim what was once an industrial site: meadows, woods and wetlands now replace industry, and are linked by a series of paths developed for quiet recreation and educational use. The park is managed by Carmarthenshire County Council, supported by volunteers from the Friends of Ynys Dawela and open for anyone to enjoy. Daniel Williams wrote about this spot in his 1865 essay, lamenting how the 'island' in the river was once covered by flowers and had sheep and cattle grazing there, but had been replaced by a 'river of boiling fire' and 'holes leading to underground cells'.[2] How happy he would be to know flowers grow once more and all is peaceful.

Writing this account about the Black Mountain road, the two John Joneses and Brynaman, has been a fascinating journey, just like driving the road itself is a great experience. This work has not attempted to provide an extensive history of the area but, rather, to give a glimpse of its fascinating history, and how two men moved the Industrial Revolution forward in what was once a remote part of Wales. Any information that anyone feels I have neglected, I apologise, as I also do if there is anything that I have included which is incorrect. My aim was to bring together, in one place, fragments of information from various sources, places and people, to illustrate why and how the road over the mountain was built, and its importance in developing the area.

Endnotes

Preface

1 William Blake (1757–1827), 'Gnomic Verses', first line, *c.*1806–1810.

2 Jones D.R. & Jones G.A., *In the Mist of Time* (2005), to be found at West Glamorgan Archives (Ref. D/D Z 620/1).

3 Williams, Daniel, 'Hanes y Gwterfawr, ei thrigolion, eu masnach, a'u crefydd or flwyddyn 1800 hyd diwedd 1860' (1865, NLW MS 22031A).

Chapter 1: Pre-industrial history

1 http://www.coflein.gov.uk/en/site/309913/details/capel-gwynfe.

2 Turner's *Hereford Court Sketchbook* (Tate D01267–D01270, D01341; Turner Bequest XL 17–20, 87), Tate Britain, London.

3 Evans, G.E., 'A great history of a great county', *Antiquities of Carmarthen (1834–36)*, Vol. XXVI, p.76.

4 Morgan, D.E., 'Black Mountain / Mynydd Du Survey', *Archaeology in Wales*, Vol. 28, 1988, Vols 1–4, 1905–9, pp.41–3.

5 http://www.genuki.org.uk/big/wal/GLA/Llangiwg/Gwauncaegurwen/manor.

6 freepages.history.rootsweb.ancestry.com/~cwmgors/TimeLine.

7 An advert in *The Cambrian* newspaper in 1884 notes that Brynbrain Farm will be sold with 'all mineral rights included'.

8   Davies, J., *A History of Wales* (1990), p.402.
9   Davies, J.H., *The History of Pontardawe and District* (1967), p.27.
10 Owen, J.D., Jones, J.D. & Davies B., *Hanes Eglwys Cwmllynfell* (1935), p.192.
11 Borrow, G., *Wild Wales: Its People, Language and Scenery* (1955 edition), p.481.
12 *The Black Mountain Lime Industry* (2014), Dyfed Archaeological Trust publication, available at: www.dyfedarchaeology.org.uk/calch/news2014.html.
13 Fforest Fawr Geopark information: www.fforestfawrgeopark.org.uk.

Chapter 2: The Story of the Road

1   http://www.topgear.com/car-news/the-great-outdoors/these-are-the-best-driving-roads-in-wales#3.
2   Rees, E., *Hanes Brynaman 1819–1896* (1992 edition), p.51.
3   MacPherson, G., *Highway and Transportation Engineering and Planning* (1993), p.28.
4   Webb, S. & Webb, B., *English Local Government: The Parish and the County* (1963), p.4.
5   Taylor, Thomas, *The Principality of Wales Exactly Described* (1718), National Library of Wales, Ref. Ab5212.
6   *Britannia Depicta* (1720) printed by Emanuel Bowen & John Owen, Facsimile Reprint (1970), Ward & Son Publishers; Christopher Saxton's map, National Library of Wales Map Ref 5360/1; Johannes Blaeu's *County of Glamorgan* map, West Glamorgan Archives, 1645 Map; Turnpike Trust map, Carmarthen Library, Reference Map 65; John Cowley's 1744 map of Carmarthenshire, National Library of Wales Map Collection, 6610; Humphrey Lloyd's map: article by Prof Huw Pryce reproduced in *Western Mail* 25/8/2018, 'The Renaissance scholar who drew Wales on the global stage'.
7   Moore-Colyer, Richard J., *Welsh Cattle Drovers* (1976), p.97.
8   Copeland, J., *Roads and their Traffic 1750–1850* (1968), p.62.

9   Duckham, Baron F., 'Road Administration in South Wales: The Carmarthenshire Roads Board 1845–89', *Journal of Transport History*, 5(1): 45–65, March 1984.

10 http://www.parliament.uk/about/living-heritage/ transformingsociety/transportcomms/roadsrail/overview/ turnpikestolls/.

11 Schlee, Duncan & Pritchard, Huw & Page, Marion, 'Turnpike and Pre-Turnpike Roads', Dyfed Archaeological Trust website (2016); Beechsquirrel, Nicola, 'Lime, Tolls, Roads and Rebecca', at http://www.dyfedarchaeology.org.uk/calch/ rebeccariots.pdf.

12 Duckham, Baron F., 'Road Administration in South Wales: The Carmarthenshire Roads Board 1845–89', *Journal of Transport History*, 5(1): 45–65, March 1984.

13 Albert, W., *The Turnpike Road System In England 1663–1840* (1972), pp.57–119.

14 Rees, Lowri Ann, 'Paternalism and rural protest: the Rebecca Riots', http://www.bahs.org.uk/AGHR/ARTICLES/59_1_3_ Rees.pdf.

15 Williams, D., *Rebecca Riots: A Study in Agrarian Discontent* (1955), pp.272–91, 447–8.

16 Sir John Williams Deeds and Papers: Petition of the Trustees and Creditors of the Llandovery and Llangadock Turnpike Trust *c.*1840, National Library of Wales.

17 Evans, M.C.S., 'Forgotten Roads of Carmarthen', *Carmarthenshire Antiquarian*, Vols 20–22 1984–6, pp.33–47.

18 Albert, W., *The Turnpike Road System in England, 1663–1840* (1972), pp.94–118.

19 Jones D.R. & Jones G.A., *In the Mist of Time* (2005) available at West Glamorgan Archives (Ref. D/D Z 620/1), p.74.

20 Evans, M.C.S., 'Forgotten Roads of Carmarthen', *Carmarthenshire Antiquarian*, Vols 20–22 1984–6, pp.33–47.

21 Plan of intended line of road, John Williams, 27 November 1830, Glamorgan Archives, Ref. O/D/P/43, deposited plans, 1792-197.

22 Rees, E., *Hanes Brynaman 1819–1896* (1992 edition), p.19.

23 Sir John Williams Deeds and Papers: Petition of the Trustees and Creditors of the Llandovery and Llangadock Turnpike Trust *c.*1840, National Library of Wales, Ref. B11/86.

24 Reader, W.J., *Macadam: The McAdam Family and the Turnpike Roads 1798–1861* (1980); Ransom, P.J.G., *The Archaeology of the Transport Revolution 1750–1850* (1984); McAdam, John, *Observations on the Highways of the Kingdom* (1816); *Remarks on the Present System of Road Making...* (1816); *Observations on the Management of Trusts of the Care of Turnpike Roads...* (1825).

25 Carmarthen Archives, collection reference TT Box v/2.

26 Ibid.

27 Duckham, Baron F., 'Road Administration in South Wales: The Carmarthenshire Roads Board 1845–89', *Journal of Transport History*, 5(1): 45–65, March 1984.

28 Reader, W.J., *Macadam: The McAdam Family and the Turnpike Roads 1798–1861* (1980), pp.37–8. Appendix to Chapter 2 reproduces part of McAdam's Report to the Select Committee on Highways and Turnpike Roads, 1810–11.

29 Ibid., p.38.

30 Carmarthen Archives, Reference TT BOX ii/9, receipts, September 1839.

31 Carmarthen Archives, Reference TT Box ii/8.

32 Carmarthen Archives, Reference TT BOX ii/9, receipts, September 1839.

33 Carmarthen Archives, Reference TT Box iii/1, copy of 1784 Turnpike Act.

34 Evan, D.A. and Walters, H.W., *Amman Valley Long Ago / Dyffryn Aman 'Slawer Dydd* (1987), p.2.

35 Duckham, Baron F., 'Road Administration in South Wales: The Carmarthenshire Roads Board 1845–89', *Journal of Transport History*, 5(1): 45–65, March 1984.

36 Evans, M.C.S., 'Forgotten Roads of Carmarthen', *Carmarthenshire Antiquarian*, Vols 20–22, 984–6, p.40.

Chapter 3: John Jones Brynbrain – Father and Son

1   National Library of Wales (NLW) Ref: SD 1835-165.
2   Jones D.R. & Jones G.A., *In the Mist of Time* (2005) available at West Glamorgan Archives (Ref. D/D Z 620/1).
3   http://freepages.rootsweb.com/~cwmgors/history/Waun. html#Photographs Picture Gallery, Brynaman Silver Band Collection.
4   'Farm Survey Report: Bryn Llefrith, Cwmllynfell', *Historic Farm Buildings Group*, 1 (1987), pp.31–34, http://www.hfbg. org.uk/images/HFBGJournal1987-2003.pdf.
5   *Y Tyst a'r Dydd*, 4 Rhagfyr [December] 1877.
6   Thomas, H., 'The Industrialization of a Glamorgan Parish', *National Library of Wales Journal*, Winter 1976, Volume XIX/4, p.359.
7   Owen, J.D., Jones, J.D. & Davies B., *Hanes Eglwys Cwmllynfell* (1935), p.36.
8   West Glamorgan Archives, Ref: D/D SB 13/3. Mortgage document security all the lands known as Gwter Fawr.
9   West Glamorgan Archives, Ref: D/D SB 13/6. Edinburgh Life Insurance document, 3 October 1846.
10 Wolmar, Christian, *Fire and Steam: A New History of the Railways in Britain* (2008), pp.86–112, 121–2, 143–6.
11 *London Gazette*, 19 April 1859, p.1656.
12 Rees, E., *Hanes Brynaman 1819–1896* (1992 edition), p.27.
13 Walters, H., *Canu'r Pwll a'r Pulpud* (1987), p.80.
14 West Glamorgan Archives, Ref: D/D SB 13/E/1. *Book of Maps and Sales Particulars*, Jonah Jones Land and Mineral Surveyor for the Amman Iron Company (1857).
15 Rees, E., *Hanes Brynaman 1819–1896* (1896), p.37. His earlier 1883 publication *Hanes Brynaman o'r flwyddyn 1820–1881* available at the National Library of Wales.
16 Ibid., p.37.

Chapter 4: Industrialisation of Brynaman

1   Davies, J.H., *The History of Pontardawe and District* (1967), p.103.
2   'The Coal Industry 1750–1914', *Glamorgan County History, Volume V, Industrial Glamorgan from 1700 to 1970* (1980).
3   Williams, Daniel, 'Hanes y Gwterfawr, ei thrigolion, eu masnach, a'u crefydd or flwyddyn 1800 hyd diwedd 1860' (1865). Unpublished essay available at National Library of Wales, Ref: Facs 215.
4   Rees, D., *Carmarthenshire the Concise History* (2006), p.127.
5   http://llangadog.com/history.html.
6   Rees, D., *Carmarthenshire the Concise History* (2006), p.117.
7   Thomas, H., 'The Industrialization of a Glamorgan Parish', *National Library of Wales Journal*, 1975, Volume XIX/2, pp.345–61.
8   Labour Congress, London, 1891. Enoch Rees's testimony on behalf of the Anthracite Coal Regions of South Wales. https://freepages.rootsweb.com/~cwmgors/history/BrynammanCoal.html).
9   'An Eton Schoolboy Visits the Amman Valley: Diary of a Public Schoolboy', *Carmarthenshire Antiquary*, Volume XL (2004).
10 National Archives, Ref: MT 6/33/10. Correspondence of the Llanelly Railway & Dock Company relating to Brynaman, 1863 (Rail 355 & 377).
11 Page, J., *Forgotten Railways – South Wales* (1979), p.124.
12 Rees, E., *Hanes Brynaman 1819–1896* (1896), pp.36–7, 78.
13 Davies, J., *A History of Wales* (1990), p.398.
14 Thomas, Brinley, *Migration and Urban Development* (1972), pp.170–81.
15 Rees, E., *Hanes Brynaman 1819–1896* (1992 edition), p.115.
16 Price, Rhys and Griffiths, E., *Y Llysieu-lyfr Teuluaidd* (1890 edition).
17 Ibid., pp.185, 215.
18 Ibid., pp.183–5.

19 Michael, Pamela, 'Public Health in Wales (1800–2000) A brief history', http://www.wales.nhs.uk/documents/ 090203historypublichealthen%5B1%5D.pdf.

20 http://freepages.rootsweb.com/~cwmgors/history/Schools. html; https://www.dyfedfhs.org.uk/cmn-schools.

21 Rees, D., *Carmarthenshire the Concise History* (2006), p.79.

22 Rees, E., *Hanes Brynaman 1819–1896* (1896) and his earlier 1883 publication *Hanes Brynaman o'r flwyddyn 1820–1881* available at the National Library of Wales, p.77.

23 *Glo Mân: Papur Bro Dyffryn Aman*, Rhif/No. 329, Mai 2010, p.1.

24 Thomas, E., *Dathlu Canmlwyddiant Clwb Rugbi Brynaman The Village and its Rugby* (1998), p.57.

25 Ibid., p.52.

26 Rees, E., *Hanes Brynaman 1819–1896* (1992 edition), p.111–17.

27 Davies, J.H., *The History of Pontardawe and District* (1967). p.89.

28 Labour Congress, London, 1891. English version available at http://freepages.rootsweb.com/~cwmgors/history/. BrynammanCoal.html and original in Welsh in Enoch Rees's *Hanes Brynaman* (1896).

29 Morris, J.H. & Williams, L.J., *The South Wales Coal Industry 1841–1875* (1958), p.219.

30 Williams, Daniel, 'Hanes y Gwterfawr, ei thrigolion, eu masnach, a'u crefydd or flwyddyn 1800 hyd diwedd 1860' (1865). Unpublished essay available at National Library of Wales, Ref: Facs 215.

31 Rees, E., *Hanes Brynaman 1819–1896* (1992 edition), p.13.

32 Davies, J., *A History of Wales* (1990), p.403.

33 Owen, J.D., Jones, J.D. & Davies B., *Hanes Eglwys Cwmllynfell* (1935), p.174.

34 Rees, E., *Hanes Brynaman 1819–1896* (1992 edition), p.122.

35 Borrow, G., *Wild Wales: Its People, Language and Scenery* (1955 edition), p.488.

36 Jones, M.H., *Hanes Siloam Brynaman* (1972), p.32.

37 Rees, E., *Hanes Brynaman 1819–1896* (1992 edition), p.42.
38 Ibid., p.46.
39 Davies, J., *A History of Wales* (1990), p.403.
40 Williams, Daniel, 'Hanes y Gwterfawr, ei thrigolion, eu masnach, a'u crefydd or flwyddyn 1800 hyd diwedd 1860' (1865). Unpublished essay available at National Library of Wales, Ref: Facs 215.

Chapter 5: Brynaman's social, religious and cultural development

1   Thomas, H., 'The Industrialization of a Glamorgan Parish', *National Library of Wales Journal*, 1975, Volume XIX/2, pp.345–61.
2   Borrow, G., *Wild Wales: Its People, Language and Scenery* (1955 edition), p.490.
3   Rees, D., *Carmarthenshire the Concise History* (2006), p.128.
4   Rees, Enoch, Labour Congress report, London, 1891, in *Hanes Brynaman* (1896), p.144.
5   Morris, J.H. & Williams, L.J., *The South Wales Coal Industry 1841–1875* (1958), p.236.
6   Owen, D. Huw, *The Chapels of Wales* (2012), p.13.
7   Jones, J. Gwynfor, 'Reflections on the religious revival in Wales 1904–05', *Journal of the United Reformed Church History Society*, 7.7 (2005), pp.427–45.
8   Morris, J.H. & Williams, L.J., *The South Wales Coal Industry 1841–1875* (1958), pp.128–9.
9   Royal Commissions, Trades' Union Report, 1867–8.
10 West Glamorgan Archives, Ref. D/D Xfd 1 (1754).
11 Owen, J.D., Jones, J.D. & Davies B., *Hanes Eglwys Cwmllynfell* (1935), pp.1–22.
12 *Glo Mân: Papur Bro Dyffryn Aman*, Chwefror 1985.
13 Thomas, E., *Dathlu Canmlwyddiant Clwb Rugbi Brynaman The Village and its Rugby* (1998), p.103.
14 Hilton George W., *The Truck System, Including a History of the British Truck Acts, 1465–1960* (1960), pp.xii, 166.

15 *Kelly's Directory for Monmouth and South Wales*, 1891, available at Swansea Central Library.

16 www.treftadaethbrynamman-heritage.org.uk.

17 Thomas, E., *Dathlu Canmlwyddiant Clwb Rugbi Brynaman The Village and its Rugby* (1998), pp.53–4.

18 Reynolds, P., *The Ironmasters' Bags: The postal service in the South Wales Valleys c.1760–c.1860* (2010), pp.33–36. See also Evans, G.E., 'A Great History of a Great County', *Antiquities of Carmarthen (1834–36)*, Volume XXVI, available at Carmarthen Library.

19 Robert Rowe, *A new map of England and Wales describing all the Turnpike and Principle Bye Roads*, 1819, British Library Reference Maps, 1175 (45).

20 Davies, J.H., *The History of Pontardawe and District* (1967), pp.218–19.

21 Jenkins, G.H. (ed.) *The Welsh Language and its Social Domains, 1801–1911*, (2000), pp.431–57.

22 Rees, E., *Hanes Brynaman 1819–1896* (1992 edition), pp.113–19.

23 Jenkins, G.H. (ed.) *The Welsh Language and its Social Domains, 1801–1911*, (2000), pp.431–57.

24 Thomas, Hugh, 'The Industrialization of a Glamorgan Parish', *National Library of Wales Journal*, Winter 1976, Volume XIX/4, pp.345–61.

25 Rhianydd Morgan, 'Sain, Cerdd a Chân ym Mrynaman' in Hywel Teifi Edwards's (ed.) *Cwm Aman* (1996).

26 http://www.brynammancinema.org/history.

27 The *Amman Valley Chronicle* and *East Carmarthen News*, 16 December 1915, have detailed accounts of this event.

28 *Eglwys Annibynnol Bethania, Rhosaman, Canmlwyddiant 1905–2005*. Book published to celebrate 100 years of Bethania Chapel (2005), p.35.

29 Rees, E., *Hanes Brynaman 1819–1896* (1992 edition), p.37.

30 Jones, Marian Henry, *Hanes Siloam Brynaman* (1972), pp. 20–37.

31 Borrow, G., *Wild Wales: Its People, Language and Scenery* (1955 edition), pp.482–8.
32 Rees, D., *Carmarthenshire the Concise History* (2006), p. 138.

Chapter 6: Conclusion

1   William Blake (1757–1827), 'Gnomic Verses', first line, *c.*1806–1810.
2   Williams, Daniel, 'Hanes y Gwterfawr, ei thrigolion, eu masnach, a'u crefydd or flwyddyn 1800 hyd diwedd 1860' (1865). Unpublished essay to be found at National Library of Wales (NLW MS 22031A).

Bibliography

Albert, W., *The Turnpike Road System In England 1663–1840* (1972).
Borrow, G., *Wild Wales: Its People, Language and Scenery* (1862).
Copeland, J., *Roads and their Traffic 1750–1850* (1968).
Davies, J., *A History of Wales* (1990).
Davies, J.H., *History of Pontardawe and District* (1967).
Evan, D.A. and Walters, H.W., *Amman Valley Long Ago / Dyffryn Aman 'Slawer Dydd* (1987).
Evans, M.C.S., 'Forgotten Roads of Carmarthen', *Carmarthenshire Antiquarian*, Vols 20–22 1984–6.
Evans, Prof. Myron W., *O Hudd Ei Ddoe* (2012).
Hugh, T., 'The Industrialization of a Glamorgan Parish', *National Library of Wales Journal*, Vol. XIX/2 Winter 1975, Vol. XIX/3 Summer 1976 & Vol. XIX/4 Winter 1976.
Jones D.R. & Jones G.A., *In the Mist of Time* (2005) available at West Glamorgan Archives (Ref. D/D Z 620/1).
Moore-Colyer, Richard J., *Welsh Cattle Drovers* (1976).
Morris, J.H. & Williams, L.J., *The South Wales Coal Industry 1841–1875* (1958).
Owen, D. Huw, *The Chapels of Wales* (2012).
Owen, J.D., Jones, J.D. & Davies B., *Hanes Eglwys Cwmllynfell* (1935).

Page, James, *Forgotten Railways: South Wales* (1979).

Price, Rhys and Griffiths, E., *Y Llysieu-lyfr Teuluaidd* (3rd edition, 1890). A copy of the first edition is available at the British Library. Pryce's name was Anglicized to Price on all editions.

Prys-Jones, A.G., *The Story of Carmarthenshire – From Prehistoric Times to the beginning of the Sixteenth Century*, Vol. I (1959) & *The Story of Carmarthenshire – From the Sixteenth Century to 1832*, Vol. II (1972).

Rees, D., *Carmarthenshire the Concise History* (2006).

Rees, E., *Hanes Brynaman 1819–1896* (1896) and his earlier 1883 publication *Hanes Brynaman o'r flwyddyn 1820–1881* available at the National Library of Wales. Page references are for the 1992 edition.

Thomas, E., *Dathlu Canmlwyddiant Clwb Rugbi Brynaman The Village and its Rugby* (1998).

Thomas, B., *Migration and Urban Development* (1972).

Williams, D., *Rebecca Riots: A Study in Agrarian Discontent* (1955).

Other sources

Hicks, G., at www.genuki.org.uk/big/wal/CMN/providers

1804–1919 newspapers: https://newspapers.library.wales.

1841–1910 censuses available at libraries and online websites.

Book of Maps and Sales particulars by Jonah Jones Land and Mineral Surveyor for the Amman Iron Company (1857) Permission granted by West Glamorgan Archives Services Ref DD SB13/E/1.

Trade Directories available at Swansea Library.

Appendix I:

Timeline of development

Dates for significant buildings, trade and industry to the south of the Black Mountain road. This is how Brynaman developed in the context of significant historical events.

1600s   Small-scale mining starts

1751–72   Turnpike trusts in area start building roads

1760   Industrial Revolution begins and last until mid-1840s
At the start of the 19th century there is no village on the south side of the Black Mountain

1800s   Only 21 dwellings in Gwter Fawr area (farmhouses, cottages and crofts)

1802   John Jones opens a mine in Blaengurwen, Rhosaman

1819   John Jones opens Lefel yr Office Colliery in Gwter Fawr, south of the River Amman, and builds the first row of miners' cottages near the works later buried under Pencraig tip

1819   Black Mountain road is built from Gwter Fawr to quarries

1819   Bridge built by John Jones over the River Amman near the present location of the Farmers' Arms / rugby club

1820   Tollgate opens in Gwter Fawr

1823   Farmers' Arms built near Gwter Fawr Colliery

1824–31   Black Mountain road extended towards Gwaun-Cae-Gurwen

1824–31   First shop opened by Twm o'r Gat

1824–31	First small-scale schools start being held in different houses
1837	Victorian era begins
1837–9	'Old Pit' in Gwaun-Cae-Gurwen succeeds in reaching the Big Vein and full industrialisation begins
1838	Brynaman House built, with the area's first slate roof
1838	Second pub opens – the Colliers' Arms on Park Street
1839	Watkins' shop, a grocer and draper, built – second slate roof on Station Road
1839–43	Rebecca Riots
1840	Railway mania
1840	New Farmers' Arms pub is built near the bridge across the River Amman. Third slate roof in area.
1840	Sunday school starts at various unknown locations
1842	Gibea is the first chapel to be built
1842	First railway comes as far as the turnpike road that leads up to the Black Mountain road (now known as Station Road) on the opposite side of the river to the New Farmers' Arms. By the mid-1840s there are two shops, four pubs, one chapel, but no school, and the population is now around 300.
1844	Turnpike trusts abolished
1847	Amman Iron Company opens near the bridge that crosses the River Amman and where the two county boundaries meet. Mr Llywelyn buys Gwter Fawr mine from John Jones, then builds two blast furnaces.
1847	Mr Llywelyn builds houses for his workers
1847	The Crown pub is built on Brynaman Road
1848	More houses built for workforce: 20 above the station (Hall Street today), five on Station Road and an unrecorded number on Cwmgarw Road
1850	Company Truck shop opens (exact location unknown)
1851	Mr Llywelyn opens a new forge
1854	George Borrow describes Gwter Fawr as one long street with some scattered houses. A terrace of

cottages, just off Bryn Road (the old turnpike road), is built around this period.

1856   First school opens in Gibea and a new bigger chapel is built.

By 1860 private houses have been built, the total now being 146. The population is approximately 850.

1861   A bigger forge is built at the Amman ironworks

1864   Second railway arrives just below Brynaman House and 'Brynaman' Station opens. Passenger service starts.

1865   Tregib Arms built on Cwmgarw Road. Company Truck shop closes.

1866   Brynaman Post Office opens. Village is now officially known as Brynaman.

1868   New school built at bottom of the Black Mountain road, opposite Gibea Chapel

1868   Third furnace is built – known as the 'Big Furnace'

1868   Gwyn Arms opens on Cwmgarw Road

1868   First passenger train on the Midland line arrives in Brynaman

1871   Moriah Chapel on Cwmgarw Road is the second chapel built

1872   Siloam Chapel built on Banwen Common

1872   Tinplate works opens on the Carmarthenshire side of the river Amman

1872   Twenty houses built by Mr Strick for his workers in a road known as Tinmen's Row; road later renamed to Chapel Street

1873   Ynys Colliery opened in Brynaman by the Welsh Company and a quarry opened above Cwmllynfell by John Hay

1873   Twenty houses built both sides of Cannon Road, towards Gwaun-Cae-Gurwen

1874   Twenty cottages built for tin workers on Coedcae Hopkin. Strick's company had built a total of 82 houses for its workforce by this date.

1876	Co-op shop opens
1880	Development of continental trade of coal by the owners of Gwaun-Cae-Gurwen Colliery, Frederick and Charles Cleeves
1880–1	St Catherine's Church built opposite to Gibea Chapel, but off the main road
1882	Ebenezer Chapel is built on Amman Road
1885–6	Waterworks built, supplying 112 private houses and 28 communal roadside taps
1889	Branch of Glamorganshire Bank opens on Station Road
1890	Glynbeudy tinplate works opens.

By the 1890s there were 380 private houses, approximately 30 shops as well as a chemist, tailor, blacksmith, stonemason, carpenter, seven pubs and a coffee tavern, four chapels and one school. Population has grown to 2,000.

1894	Brynaman Hotel is built to replace the Old Farmers' Arms.
1896	Another school opens in Lower Brynaman, Ysgol y Glyn
1901	Victorian era ends.

By 1903 the list of shops and traders had been added to, with two china shops, three confectioners, two more coffee taverns, an insurance company and newsagent, as well as two solicitors.

1904	Electricity arrives; first building with electricity is Gibea Chapel
1905	Bethania Chapel built in Rhosaman
1909	Hermon Chapel is built on Brynaman Road, on the edge of Gwaun-Cae-Gurwen Common
1914–18	First World War
1924	Brynaman Public Hall and cinema opens.

In the 1950s railways, quarries and other industries started to close.

Glossary of place names

Original Welsh names and spellings for the villages have mainly been used

Brynaman's English spelling is Brynamman

Gwter Fawr is sometimes spelt as one word, Gwterfawr, and in some old English texts as Gutter Vawr

Gwaun-Cae-Gurwen: old spelling is Kaegurwen

Gwynfe: old spelling Gwinfe or Gwinvey Chapel, as seen on old maps

Llangadog: Welsh spelling is used, apart from when Llangadock Turnpike Trust is referred to in the text as most archive material has the English spelling

River Amman: on old maps it is noted as Amon, Welsh spelling Aman

Neyadd Wen: old spelling is Noyadd Wen

Tywi: Towy is the English spelling

Grid References for some locations

Brynaman House: SN 71290 13968

Brynaman tollhouse: SN 71398 14326

Brynbrain Farm: SN 74686 13510

Carreg Cennen Castle: SN 66741 19130

Cwmllynfell Old Chapel: SN 74665 12355

Gwynfe: SN 72259 21977

Hen Bethel: SN 68270 14385

Milestones: Tro'r Derlwyn SN 72483 15722 and listed milestone in
Lower Brynaman SN 70924 13559

Old turnpike road: Bryn Road SN 71301 14988 northwards to
SN 70762 19343

Quarries: SN 73558 18923

Sylfaen Stone (Carreg Sylfaen): SN 70718 12500

Tro'r Gwcw: SN 72465 19351

APPENDIX III

Jones family tree

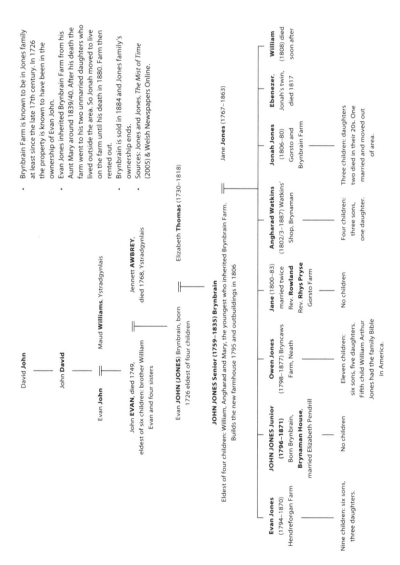

- Brynbrain Farm is known to be in Jones family at least since the late 17th century. In 1726 the property is known to have been in the ownership of Evan John.
- Evan Jones inherited Brynbrain Farm from his Aunt Mary around 1839/40. After his death the farm went to his two unmarried daughters who lived outside the area. So Jonah moved to live on the farm until his death in 1880. Farm then rented out.
- Brynbrain is sold in 1884 and Jones family's ownership ends.
- Sources: Jones and Jones, *The Mist of Time* (2005) & Welsh Newspapers Online.

David John

John **David**

Evan **John** ⚭ Maud **Williams**, Ystradgynlais

John **EVAN**, died 1749,
eldest of six children: brother William
Evan and four sisters

Jennett **AWBREY**,
died 1768, Ystradgynlais

Evan **JOHN (JONES)** Brynbrain, born
1726 eldest of four children

Elizabeth **Thomas** (1730–1818)

JOHN JONES Senior (1759–1835) Brynbrain
Eldest of four children: William, Angharad and Mary, the youngest who inherited Brynbrain Farm.
Builds the new farmhouse 1795 and outbuildings in 1806

Jane **Jones** (1767–1863)

Evan Jones
(1794–1870)
Hendreforgan Farm

JOHN JONES Junior
(1796–1871)
Born Brynbrain,
Brynaman House,
married Elizabeth Pendrill

Owen Jones
(1798–1877) Bryncaws
Farm, Neath

Jane (1800–83)
married twice
Rev. **Rowland**
Rev. **Rhys Pryse**
Gorsto Farm

Angharad Watkins
(1802/3–1887) Watkins'
Shop, Brynaman

Jonah Jones
(1806–80)
Gorsto and
Brynbrain Farm

Ebenezer,
Jonah's twin,
died 1817

William
(1808) died
soon after

Nine children: six sons,
three daughters.

No children

Eleven children:
six sons, five daughters.
Fifth child William Arthur
Jones had the family Bible
in America.

No children

Four children:
three sons,
one daughter.

Three children: daughters
two died in their 20s. One
married and moved out
of area.

APPENDIX IV

Diagram of Black Mountain area

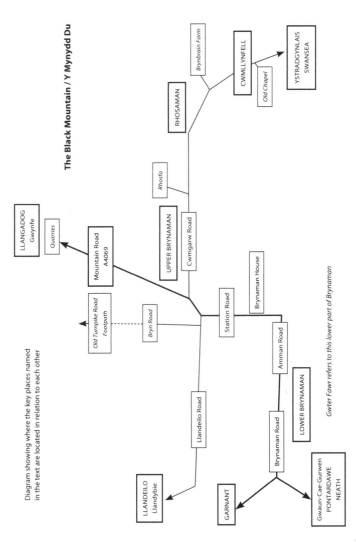

Diagram showing where the key places named in the text are located in relation to each other

The Black Mountain / Y Mynydd Du

LLANGADOG Gwynfe

Quarries

Mountain Road A4069

Old Turnpike Road Footpath

Bryn Road

UPPER BRYNAMAN

Cwmgarw Road

Rhosfa

RHOSAMAN

Brynbrain Farm

CWMLLYNFELL

Old Chapel

YSTRADGYNLAIS SWANSEA

Station Road

Brynaman House

Llandeilo Road

Amman Road

LOWER BRYNAMAN

Gwter Fawr refers to this lower part of Brynaman

LLANDEILO Llandybie

Brynaman Road

GARNANT

Gwaun-Cae-Gurwen PONTARDAWE NEATH

127

Diagram of Brynaman

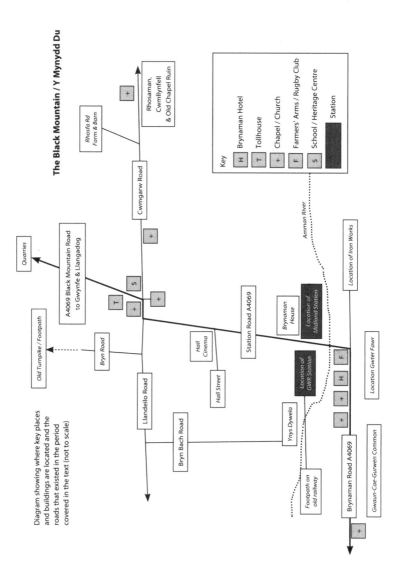

The Black Mountain / Y Mynydd Du

Diagram showing where key places and buildings are located and the roads that existed in the period covered in the text (not to scale)

Key

H	Brynaman Hotel
T	Tollhouse
+	Chapel / Church
F	Farmers' Arms / Rugby Club
S	School / Heritage Centre
	Station

Rhosfa Rd Farm & Barn

Rhosaman, Cwmllynfell & Old Chapel Ruin

Cwmgarw Road

A4069 Black Mountain Road to Gwynfe & Llangadog

Quarries

Old Turnpike / Footpath

Bryn Road

Llandeilo Road

Bryn Bach Road

Hall Street

Hall Cinema

Station Road A4069

Brynaman House

Location of Midland Station

Amman River

Location of Iron Works

Location Gwter Fawr

Ynys Dywela

Location of GWR Station

Footpath on old railway

Brynaman Road A4069

Gwaun-Cae-Gurwen Common